Jerome Teelucksingh

Awesome Americans

Jerome Teelucksingh

Awesome Americans

and some not so awesome

JustFiction Edition

Imprint

Cover image: www.ingimage.com

Publisher:
JustFiction! Edition
is a trademark of
Dodo Books Indian Ocean Ltd. and OmniScriptum S.R.L publishing group

120 High Road, East Finchley, London, N2 9ED, United Kingdom
Str. Armeneasca 28/1, office 1, Chisinau MD-2012, Republic of Moldova, Europe
Printed at: see last page
ISBN: 978-620-6-74140-4

Dedicated to migrants in North America

Table of Contents

Surviving....5
Time to move on....13
Talented and gifted....29
Coping with problems....45
Return to the Caribbean....53
Life in New York....61
Culture....71
A boring conference....83
Hoops and homecoming....99

Chapter 1
Surviving

The small, jagged red circle on his white merino began to expand. It was a circle of blood and this was the spot that the bullet had entered his chest. Ritchie stood motionless watching the writhing body on the ground. Innocent blood had desecrated the St. Barb's community. He pulled the trigger again. The body stopped moving. This was his first killing and he felt numb. He was a member of the Gambinos, a local gang that had a membership of nineteen youths. Image was important and the local gangs adopted names from abroad to enhance their local status.

It was surreal. Ritchie wore sunglasses, a thick gold chain, washed out jeans and a hoodie. He had seen hundreds of killings on television and cinema but this was reality. It was part of the gang's initiation but more importantly, it was payment for double-crossing his foreign boss. The boss lived in Colombia. He looked around to see if anyone had seen the crime then jumped into a heavily tinted car and sped off.

A Picton Squad gang member, standing near a telephone pole, witnessed the murder. News of the killing spread across the underworld. There would be repercussions.

Oh Lawd! Why he had to die! screamed Ritchie. Tears rolled down his cheeks and he looked upward. 'Why God? Why God! Bruno was too good to die!'

Aboud was polishing his car. Every Friday he washed and polished the car. On Mondays he cleaned the mats and seats. On Tuesdays, he cleaned the rims and checked the radiator. Aboud was single and spent most of his time maintaining his vehicle which was often used for drag racing. He heard the commotion and peeped over the wall. Ritchie was rolling around in the middle of the road. He opened the gate and asked a question.

Ritchie was hysterical. 'Take me instead! Why God!' He began to tear his jersey and pulled his hair. 'Why de cat? Why de cat had to die? Why?' There were eight adults and three children staring at Ritchie whose tears were streaming down his cheeks.

'Is jus' a cat…a stray cat. Yuh could get a new one,' said Aboud. He shook his head and returned to cleaning the car. He was bareback, had a thick gold chain and a gold earring.

Ritchie glared at him. 'Yuh stink and wutless! Ah fed up of all yuh uncaring people in dis street.' His four gold teeth reflected the sun's rays. His ranting continued then subsided. He went inside for ice-cream but there were no clean spoons so he used a fork. He returned outside and sat on a stool. It was hot and he greedily consumed the ice-cream. He decided to speak to Aboud.

Ritchie and Aboud lived in Crown Trace in Enterprise. This was a normal scenario in a small community in central Trinidad in the Caribbean.

'Pak, pak ah getting a heart attack,' screamed Ritchie. He dropped to the ground and held his chest. It was typical drama on Crown Trace.

Sumintra, Ritchie's aunt, heard and hurriedly packed a bag with Ritchie's clothes and toothbrush. She left the bag near his body on the road. Then, began searching the telephone directory for medical emergency numbers. She found a number and called the hospital. Two hours later the ambulance had not yet arrived. She dialled the hospital and pleaded for an ambulance. After one hour there was no response from the hospital. She told Aboud and he decided to call Dass Funeral Home. In ten minutes a hearse arrived. The driver and his assistant emerged from the vehicle.

'Listen, dis man not fully dead yet,' said Aboud, 'can you drop him off at the health centre or hospital?'

The driver and his assistant laughed and agreed. Ritchie was twitching on the ground. They carefully placed him in a brown coffin and closed the door.

Sumintra wondered if her nephew had epilepsy. 'Make sure he dead,' she murmured, 'he is a real pest in de neighbourhood…a real pest.'

Next day, Sumintra shouted to Aboud, 'Ah miss dat boy! De place doh feel de same. He was de life of the street.' She placed a hand on her forehead. 'If yuh know how ah miss dat boy! He was….' Their conversation was interrupted by a loud siren. Aboud thought it was the police. It was an ambulance. The attendants quickly jumped out and began running with a stretcher.

The driver asked, 'Somebody call de hospital yesterday for an ambulance?' It was an apologetic tone and he had a genuine look of concern. 'Yesterday we was a bit busy.'

Aboud and Sumintra were shocked at this late arrival. Aboud was furious and regained his composure. 'Don't bother, go back, we sort it out.' Both men replaced the stretcher and entered the ambulance.

Sumintra shouted, 'Allyuh is a set of good for nothing! A waste of time!' She cursed them then turned to Aboud. 'I hate this country. Nothing works properly and efficiently.'

Aboud nodded. 'Yeah me too.' He opened the hood of his car and began checking the oil and spark plugs. 'Gosh it look like ah need a new carburetor.'

Sumintra Benn was an illegal Guyanese who was married to Gadahar, an electrician. The couple spent most of the day arguing over trivial issues. They had one common trait- a love for vitamins. She would spend hours visiting pharmacies and checking online on the various benefits of vitamins. His favourite was Vitamin C.

Sumintra hurried to the Chaguanas Health Centre, in Montrose. She was gasping for breath. 'I come to see my nephew- Ritchie. Where he?' When she saw him on the bed she began to weep. 'Yuh poor thing. Look how dey have yuh suffering.' She dried her tears. 'All de neighbours from de street well miss you.'

He remained expressionless and listened to her. After five days he was discharged and returned home. One week later, Aboud was distressed. Someone had stolen his car. He made a report at the police station and returned to Crown Trace. Ritchie helped Aboud search for the missing car.

Ritchie went to other streets in Enterprise telling persons about the lost car. He returned to Crown Trace and saw Aboud sitting on a bench near the playground. 'I spend the whole day telling people about de lost car. Ah sure we go find it soon.' He had a sympathetic look.

Aboud felt relieved. He began to believe that Ritchie was not really bad. 'Thanks so much. I cannot sleep good dese nights. Hear na, yuh hear about de killing las' week in St. Barb's?'

Ritchie nonchalantly replied, 'Yeah, people killing cause dey need to eat ah food. Dey hungry. Ah hear it was a police killing and when de people protests de police come and use tear gas to scatter de crowd.'

'De talk on de ground is dat somebody from we street was involved. Two homeys from Second Caledonia in Morvant came to check we street.'

'Really?' Ritchie watched his facial expressions. 'Dem gang leaders causing real trouble for poor people. Dey killing leaders sometimes cause business on de block slow and dey want another drug turf. Some of dem youths killing for fun. Others for rank….'

Aboud nodded. 'Yea, is ah ranking thing.' He was a former gang member of the G-Unit. 'I glad ah give up dat life. Right now ah seriously thinking 'bout going foreign.'

Three weeks later, the police raided Ritchie's home and found parts of a car. Aboud identified the door, steering wheel and trunk as part of his car.

Sumintra was shocked. 'Dat boy is mad. He steal yuh car and helping yuh look for it!'

'I carrying him to court.' Aboud was disgusted with Ritchie's behaviour.

'By de way yuh hear a young trini in Florida gone to jail because try to steal an aeroplane?'

He chuckled. 'No, ah don't believe dat. He should be satisfied to steal a bicycle or car…but ah whole plane! Dat is pushing it too far!'

'Anyway, ah going to buy some provisions, we go talk later.' She hopped into a taxi and headed for the Chaguanas Market.

Ritchie spent one year in jail for the theft. He returned to Crown Trace and behaved as if he was innocent. He would occasionally have a bath on his front lawn. All he needed was a hose and bar of blue soap. These entertaining showers would range from ten minutes to one hour and he would be wearing either a short pants or underwear. Whilst bathing he would be loudly singing a calypso, hymn or carol. The green hose was his microphone and he did not bother about choreography. His bathing antics included sticking the hose in his ears, mouth, pants and under his arms. He enjoyed the feel of the gushing water through his hair.

Women would often visit Ritchie's home. One evening, Gadahar asked, 'Marm what business yuh have coming in Crown Trace?'

The lady was slim and wore high heels and heavy mascara. She had a blouse and a tattered jeans. 'I coming to get serviced by Ritchie.' She smiled and winked.

'Oh.' Gadahar was surprised by her frankness. 'Okay next time come a little earlier, visitors does make de dogs bark. And, remember we have a dress code in this street.' He smirked and shrugged his shoulders. He did not like these visitors. Sometimes when strange women visited Ritchie, Gadahar would light fireworks and throw them in Ritchie's yard. Ritchie would open the front door and begin to loudly curse.

Gadahar was a member of the Monster Gang. He wanted to leave but feared reprisals. He was a player with Shak Attak, a local basketball team. His team was part of the Super 10 Basketball League. Shak Attak had a good season as they were at the top of the standings. In the past five weeks they defeated Clippers, Pacers and Petro Jazz. Gadahar's cousin played for DM All Stars and tonight they had a game against Defence Force.

After receiving death threats, Ritchie wanted to leave Trinidad and Tobago. He looked at his belongings in the hall and bedroom. He decided a garage sale would be the best way to get rid of most of the items. He looked at the framed certificate on the wall. It was his most prized possession. It was the death certificate of the stray cat.

The residents of Crown Trace seemed to live in a special area that was different from the rest of Trinidad and Tobago. They lived by their own rules and laws. The police and army were afraid to drive through Crown Trace.

The sign hung from the broken gate. The letters were crooked and said- 'garbage Sale today'. Ritchie begged his neighbours to come to the garage sale. Six neighbours came and found items they had been missing after home invasions.

One of Sumintra's weaknesses was that she did not think before she spoke. Any thought or idea would be immediately discussed with whoever was closest to her. Whilst speaking she often twitched her eyes and this was due to her former drug addiction. When people spoke to her she would shrug her shoulders. It was one of her bad habits and appeared disrespectful. 'Good morning,' she said to her son.

He glanced at his mother. He was hearing impaired due to a severe ear infection. 'Stop asking me difficult questions."

She slapped his cheek. 'Boy yuh really dotish. That is not a question.' She never wanted her son to wear a hearing aid. She mollycoddled her only son.

He meekly nodded and had a frightened look.

She approached the sno-cone vendor and said, ‘Give me two sno-cones. Put plenty condensed milk in my sno-cone…not too much on the other one, is for my son who diabetic.’

The vendor nodded and pumped red syrup into the cup filled with ice. Then he let the milk drip slowly on the ice. He placed a short straw into the ice and gave the cup to her.

She paid the vendor and gave a sno-cone to her chubby son. ‘Son, eat it slowly, or else yuh belly will hurt yuh.’

The vendor smiled and adjusted his cap. ‘Of course go ahead.’ He closed his tray with ice, jumped on his bicycle and pedalled away.

Sumintra had a reputation for suing persons and institutions. She had slipped on a wet floor in a bank and sued for five million dollars. She was not pleased with the cleanliness and treatment at hospitals and sued each hospital for four million. She and her son stopped at the travel agency and checked the airfare to the United States. She disliked Trinidad and wanted to migrate. She flipped through the brochure and wondered if she could survive on social welfare checks or if her son would have to get odd jobs as washing cars or cutting lawns. She glanced at him. He was restless and was sliding on the railings.

She scolded him. ‘Boy stop that. Yuh bottom have wheels?’

He looked at her but did not understand her anger. He continued. It was an enjoyable moment.

She shouted, ‘Stop it! Splinters could damage yuh pants.’

He paused and touched the clerk’s telephone. Sumintra quickly pulled away his hand.

She roughly wiped his hand. ‘Boy why yuh so harden. If yuh dial a number I go have to pay for it. Jus’ stay quiet. Everything got COVID.’

Gadahar returned home. His shirt was soaked with sweat. It was tiring to walk eleven miles. He was a recent convert to Islam and had missed the evening prayers. On Fridays, he would attend the masjid in Longdenville. Sitting on a wooden bench near the porch was a relief. He admired the vegetable garden with the watermelon, peppers, lettuce, peas, melongene and various fruit trees. The guava tree was his prized possession but its leaves had a black fungus. The three pawpaw trees were growing near the concrete water tank and each were laden with fruit. He went inside and poured some soursop punch in a glass. It was sweet. He stirred it and returned to the porch.

There were starch and calabash mango trees. Near the cesspit was a bushy cherry tree. The cherries were juicy and sweet. He admired the sapodillas that were ready for picking. He bit into a chenette. It was not fully ripe. A dove was building a nest in the cashew tree. There were orchids, crotons and two palm trees. The cool evening breeze had stopped and there was a stillness in the air. The serenity abruptly ended.

'Yuh walk home again?' Sumintra screamed, 'I fedup tell you to take a bus if yuh too cheap to take a taxi!' She opened the gate and pushed her son inside. After locking the gate she washed her feet and hands by a tap that was near the coconut tree.

He massaged his thigh. 'Why take bus or taxi? I just save three dollars.'

'Whatever. Yuh doh lissen to nobody.' She lowered her voice. 'Shelly get kick out of her house and want to come and spend a few days here.'

He steupsed. 'What? Again? This place look like a hotel?' He winced. 'Bring some ice in a towel I want to put it on my leg.' He was glad that he had left the gang and no longer played basketball.

She went into the kitchen and returned with a towel filled with three ice cubes. 'Yes or no? Shelly want to know.'

'Is obvious the answer is no. She is a homewrecker.' He murmured, 'Is so hard being a good Muslim when it have people like Shelly and you.' His leg felt better. 'Where de boy?'

'I told him to go regular in de toilet to prevent accident,' she replied

'What stupidness yuh telling de boy! He should only go when he need to.' He called for more ice and then had an idea. 'Yuh know I feel it would be ah good business if we open a ice factory.'

She placed two blocks of ice in his hand. 'Wha' factory?'

'Ice. An ice factory!'

'Man yuh talking stupidness. Where de hell we will get de money to buy or rent a place and de ice machine expensive. Who go buy from you?' She went into the yard and checked a barbadine. It was ripe and she picked it. She heard her cellphone ringing and ignored it.

He shouted, 'Not to worry, I have an idea where to build it, it go be rel good. Everybody need ice, especially in dis hot place.'

'Whatever…is your yard.' She went into the kitchen and looked for a small knife. After peeling the barbadine, she placed the pulp in a blender and added full cream milk, sugar and condensed milk. She tasted the mixture and added more condensed milk.

During the next week he cut down all the trees and destroyed the vegetable garden. He convinced the bank to give him a loan and the money was used to buy a rusty shipping container from the port. It was rectangular and was placed in his yard. A welder made some modifications and he bought a second-hand electric motor, heating unit and valves. The ice factory worked for two days and then stopped. After extensive repairs, the factory was in operation for three days.

Sumintra and Gadahar sat in the porch staring at the container. She was in a rocking chair and he was standing staring at the red container.

'I tink we should move to de USA,' said Gadahar. He waited for her response.

She paused. 'Yeah tings not good here in Trinidad. De life much better up dere. I wasting my time living in dis community. It not progressive.'

He nodded and remained pensive.

'Dat ice generator is a rel waste of time and money,' said Sumintra, 'yuh sell any ice.'

'Is ah ice factory not a generator. I eh sell any ice yet. De machine not working properly.'

'What wrong with it?' She began cutting a half ripe mango. It was for a chow.

Gadahar was angry. 'Is jus' a little leak dat we will fix soon.'

Sumintra rolled her eyes. 'Yuh cut down all we good fruit trees and mash up de vegetable garden to build dis ice maker…ice thing….'

'Is a ice factory. Soon de leak will be found and fixed.'

'All yuh will never find dat leak. Get rid of dis ice machine before I burn it down.'

'Yuh is ah real ungrateful wretch. Ah trying so hard to earn a decent living.' He got up and went inside. He returned and reeked of expensive perfume.

She placed a spoonful of pepper sauce in the bowl of sliced mango. 'Aye where yuh going dis hour of de day?' Salt and black pepper were sprinkled on the mango pieces.

'Ah going to play some cards and dominoes with Soldier, Ritchie and Aboud. Soldier was a neighbour who worked in the Army. He had eight children and boasted that the government gave him additional allowances for each child.

The news of a virus from China caused panic in the Caribbean. In an effort to be healthier, every week Francine mixed strange potions to drink. She placed pictures of Sai Baba, Jesus and Mother Lakshmi in her kitchen. Near her bedside were copies of the Bible, Koran, Talmud and Ramayana.

One year after lockdown, the social isolation began to take a toll on Caribbean citizens. Some suffered from paranoia and hallucination. A medical quack, Terrance, did a short video that went viral on social media. He said, 'Make sure and take Eucalyptus Oil and saffron and Tea Tree Oil and place seven drops in a bucket of water. It going to work.' After swirling the water he mumbled, 'Oogabeda manea babulaba. The worse virus is the virus of sin.' The medical quackery continued as he took water from the bucket and shouted, 'This is a guaranteed cure. Sprinkle de water on yuh mouth and I get a word from de higher power for you! If yuh husband horning yuh, put some on his private parts!' The quack sneezed and wiped his nose on his sleeve. 'Don't be scared of de virus, be scared of de virus of death.'

Jestina constantly wore a mask and suffered from anxiety. She spent sleepless nights fearing the virus was a sign of the end of the world. She survived the trauma by using sleeping pills. Bertha was terrified of leaving her home. Jestina went to the market and returned with a bag filled with mauby bark. She boiled it and added spices, sugar and essence. She hoped it would strengthen her immune system.

Francine spent hours watching health updates on the television. There was a nurse from Caura Hospital being interviewed. The nurse calmly said, 'I am glad for the opportunity to communicate with the public. The coronavirus can cause mainly mild disease. Let me repeat, this is a mild disease.'

Francine shouted, 'what stupidness yuh saying? This is a serious outbreak!' She left the room to get a glass of juice. She returned and waited to hear the advice from the Minister of Health.

'This coronavirus is worse than World War One, World War Two, 9-11 and Vietnam War put together!' said the Minister of Health.

'Yes! Yes! That's correct,' shouted Francine.

Ritchie listened to Terrance's video on cures for COVID. He looked at the ads on cable television and felt he would enjoy living in the United States. Aboud also spent many hours discussing the easy life abroad. He too wanted to migrate.

Aboud and Ritchie watched the guppies in the drain. They were waiting for four friends so they could play small goal football on the road. Aboud was coughing and would occasionally clear his throat and spit in the drain. Due to their lifestyles and expensive clothing both men were known as zessers. They were seen as role models and heroes for the delinquent boys residing in Enterprise and Lendore Village.

'Ah hear rum does cure de virus,' said Ritchie.

'Good ah going for ah bottle now!'

Chapter 2
Time to move on

Jose Pico was a Venezuelan who wanted to be a novelist. He was an illegal resident in Trinidad. He had escaped the Maduro regime in 2021. He was forced to leave the city of Caracas after he lost his job as a teacher. The inflation and rising levels of poverty contributed to a mass exodus to nearby South American countries and Trinidad. He briefly worked at a car wash and his sister was a waitress in Lazy Lizard, a nightclub in Endeavour.

Mabel, Jose's wife, was an Indo-Trinidadian who had been a widow for three years. She was a former beauty queen. She had not aged gracefully and had become flabby and wrinkled. Her face was pitted and scarred and she had a brief common-law relationship with Gadahar. Mabel and Jose lived in a shack at the top of Bhadase Street in Enterprise. Both found it difficult to have a decent conversation.

Jose asked, 'What do you think about reincarnation?'

She hesitated and seemed deep in thought. 'Hmm reincarnation. I don't really drink much carnation milk, I like evaporated milk more.'

'Yes dear, me too.' Jose smiled. He sipped on a milkshake. 'What about karma?'

She thought it was an Indian delicacy. 'Yes, I love kurma, especially the fat ones that taste so good.'

Two years ago the couple migrated to United States. For five months they stayed in Paradise Inn, Springhill Suites and Sleep Inn and suites. Both enjoyed shopping in the nearby Dollar Tree. They would excitedly discuss how expensive the items would be in Venezuela or Trinidad.

In Jose's suitcase was a manuscript and he desperately wanted to get it published. Fifteen publishers rejected his manuscript and he could not afford to pay for vanity presses. This made him depressed and he began to hate the United States. He felt that if he had remained in Venezuela his work would have been appreciated and published in Spanish. Mabel would occasionally encourage him to try another publisher.

Mabel occasionally visited Target to purchase electronics, toys and household items. Her husband liked the bookstores and spent hours browsing the new titles. He entered Chapters and began checking a shelf with non-fiction books. At the back of the store was a table with cheap books. The books were not arranged neatly on the table. He glanced at the books. These were publications that once stood on shelves gathering dust. The table was the graveyard for unsold and boring books. He read the front covers which had appealing pictures and words. The words would include- 'by an international best-selling author', '#1 New York Times Bestseller', 'International Bestseller', '1 million copies in print', 'Now a major motion picture' and 'over 2 million copies sold.' Self-help books had appealing words in their titles as 'Power', 'Greatest', 'Best', 'Success', 'Leader', 'Rich' and 'How to….' These words were clichés and the books would be purchased by gullible persons. Sometimes there would be a round sticker on the front cover with the words- Winner of the Nobel Prize, Oprah's Book Club, Booker Prize, National Book Award or Winner of the Pulitzer Prize. On the back cover would be the usual praises from newspapers, obscure institutions and friends of the author. Fame and glory are only temporary. These unsold books, including classics, would eventually be thrown into the garbage as space was needed for newer and more relevant publications. The bestselling authors never knew the fate of their books that would eventually be stored in a basement or thrown into the expanding shelf of forgotten literature in a library.

'So how long have these books been on dis table?' asked Jose.

The owner had a bored look. 'The last owner had them there. Every two months I would add a few more. This is done to get more room for new titles.' He regretted having books that were unsold. He wanted a fast turnover.

'Do many people buy these books?'

'Only a few persons who feel they are getting a bargain by buying cheap books with outdated ideas and irrelevant messages. Even if I offer these books for free, people would not take them,' said the owner, 'the problem is that too many people writing.' He opened a can of Mountain Dew.

'Why do you feel people want to buy books that they would not read or enjoy?' Jose had begun to feel like a news reporter who was conducting an interview. He casually flipped through the pages of a crime novel.

'Buying a book sometimes give the feeling of power. People want others to see them leaving a bookstore with a purchase. It says something about you. On the subway and train, people are listening to audio books or reading e-books. Having knowledge and desiring knowledge are still important for some people. They might not be able to understand what they read or effectively use that knowledge to help others. Despite this they still want to have the book.'

'I realize that some people read self-help books but these books don't help them. They really need medical or professional help.'

The owner smiled. 'It's true. They read but do not absorb the essential words and miss the arguments and advice of the author. It's part of our changing culture. We expect to quickly find answers. We don't have the luxury of casually reading a book. Everything is rushed. Some people only want a free book as a gift or if they borrow it. They cheap and hate buying books.' He opened a small plastic pack and took a tablet. It was Eliquis for his heart condition. He placed it on his tongue and took a mouthful of water.

Jose saw a red clock near the store's window. It was 1.10pm. He had to return to work. He worked as a clerk at the counter of Continental Airlines at Terminal E of the George Bush International Airport in Texas. His job was to ensure the weight of each piece of luggage did not exceed the maximum limit. It was a monotonous job and lacked excitement. He felt it would have been more exciting to rummage through selected suitcases checking for contraband items.

Whilst at work various questions often crossed his mind- How would he be remembered after his death? Would he make any worthwhile contribution to society? He did not feel that his talents and experience were being fully utilized. He often felt suicidal or had the urge to kill someone. The tablets were not effective.

Mabel had earned a postgraduate degree after completion of an online course in Psychiatry offered by Extra Academic University. It was an unaccredited institution. She had a Texan accent and suffered from shingles. She diagnosed him as being bipolar. 'Jose you are bipolar but don't be worried, I recently read that a few Hollywood stars are bipolar. It's the latest trend.'

'But I want to be normal like the rest of society.'

Mabel sighed. She was serious. 'The rest of society got their problems and we don't know. It's okay to be unique and different. Who knows maybe by being different you could be a trendsetter or something like that.' He was satisfied with the answer.

Next day, Jose met his friend, Vladimir, who was a bathroom attendant for the toilets near Gate 30. Vladimir informed everyone that he was an illegal immigrant from Russia who arrived in the United States in 2002. He had a driver's license and government-issued identification card. He drove a new Ford and his wife had an Infiniti, however they both took the bus to work. His job was to ensure that toilets were flushed, liquid soap containers were refilled, mirrors wiped and the floors mopped. He was diagnosed by a psychologist and psychiatrist as being a paranoid schizophrenic and suffering from depression. For the past three years he took two tablets on a daily basis to prevent mood swings and delusions. This effort to restore his sanity was only temporary.

Jose and Vladimir would usually chat during their lunch breaks. They would buy snacks at Auntie Anne's Pretzels, and sometimes had tea or coffee at Nestle Toll House Café and Gloria Jean's Coffees. For many immigrants, United States was a country where they could find a job and food was plentiful and cheap.

In Terminal C one of the bathroom attendants was absent because she had to undergo heart surgery. The supervisor asked Vladimir to fill the temporary position which was near Gate 32. For three months he worked in this new location. On mornings he would pass near the President's Club of Continental Airlines. He longed to enter the room to use the facilities. During his morning break he would buy a copy of USA Today from CNBC News. He was always interested in reading the international news section. Sometimes he purchased a chocolate bar or nuts for his children.

During lunch-time, Vladimir ate tuna, beef, chicken or cheese sandwiches. These were prepared at home and would also be the lunches for his children, Nikita who was nine years and Ali who was twelve years old. Occasionally, he would buy lunch at the Urban Crave which boasted of selling authentic street cuisine. His favorites were braised tacos, classic burgers and chop chop salad.

For Nikita's birthday, the family spent the afternoon having dinner at El Palenque. Ali asked that he celebrate his birthday at the Golden Corral. It was Sunday and this was Ali's first buffet. His family was surprised at the large quantity of food he consumed. And, he persuaded his parents to let him experience the buffet at other Golden Corral restaurants in Texas.

During his cleaning routine, Vladimir pulled a small, yellow barrel on wheels. This barrel had mops, brooms, rags, toilet paper, liquid soap, floor deodorizer, aerosol sprays and toilet brushes. The barrel also had a small, portable yellow sign- Wet Floor. This sign would be placed on sections of the floor that were mopped. He would tell his children of incidents that he witnessed. This included stories of passengers who forgot their luggage or wristwatches in the toilet, passengers who would be reading in the toilet and who left with pieces of toilet paper stuck to their shoes. 'Today there was a man from India who forgot his yellow turban in the toilet.'

Nikita laughed and doubted the authenticity of the incident. 'You told us that already, two weeks ago.'

'No, no, no. That was an Indian man who left his suitcase behind the toilet bowl.'

Ali smiled. 'Daddy we don't believe you.' He was overweight and was regularly teased by friends and relatives.

Their father left the room and soon returned with the yellow turban which he found in the airport's toilet. Both children had shocked expressions. They laughed.

Vladimir's wife, Sumintra, was employed as a maid at the Marriott and her job was cleaning rooms. Every morning, she was given a list of rooms that needed cleaning. She was short, fat and dark-skinned. She was a graduate of the University of Guyana. She and her ex-husband, Gadahar, had one son- Ali. They divorced and she won custody of their ten year old son. They departed for the United States and overstayed their visit. Vladimir had a daughter from a brief relationship with an Irish lady.

Sumintra was an orphan. Her father shot her mother then committed suicide. This tragedy coupled with mistreatment by relatives left deep emotional scars in her life. This affected her mental health as an adult. She became delusional and wanted to create the perfect family.

One week after her first marriage, she began an adulterous relationship with Phil who was fifteen years older than her. He was light-skinned, tall and was the brother of Stetcher. Gadahar was a forgiving Muslim who tolerated his wife's ways. She was adamant that Phil was her biological dad and referred to him as dad or daddy. Initially, when Gadahar went to work, Phil would visit her home to deliver fruits, milk and roti. Three months later, Phil became bolder and on weekends would carry her to lunch, the beach and shopping. Gadahar knew of the morning and nightly visits and when they eventually met, he was obliged to call him either father-in-law or dad. The cuckolded husband often wondered if Ali was his biological son. The villagers referred to Phil by various monikers- roti man, horner man, fruit man, milkman and fake daddy.

Sumintra desperately wanted citizenship and was a fugitive from the Department of Homeland Security. She was willing to buy a fake green card and be part of a sham marriage scheme. She contacted the Very Professional Services Preparers for legal and financial assistance. However, the fee of US$8,000 was beyond her reach. She became optimistic when she received a letter in the mail. It was from Publishers Clearing House informing her that she could win US$50,000 weekly for the rest of her life. She began to daydream of the clothes and electronic items she would buy at Cyber Monday and Black Friday sales.

She met her future husband, at the airport, during one of her visits to Guyana. She had mistakenly entered the men's washroom and he smiled and told her it was the wrong place. The short conversation resulted in the exchange of telephone numbers and emails. She married him believing that she would become a U.S citizen. However, Vladimir lied about his resident status so she would marry him.

During work she collected newspapers from the tables and bins. She neatly folded each one and placed them in a green plastic bag. 'This is for recycling, I'm trying to save the environment.' Other maids did not seem to care about her efforts.

Her boss was impressed. 'I'm very glad to see that you are concerned with saving the environment.'

Sumintra was not concerned about the environment. She collected newspapers and circulars for the coupons. During the nights and weekends she would force her children to cut coupons for discounts from nearby stores. She often stole flyers from the postboxes in her neighborhood and other communities. During the nights she encouraged her husband to assist with the clipping of coupons. He would begin cutting and after fifteen minutes would complain he was bored and wanted to sleep or watch television.

Jose needed professional treatment from a psychiatrist. However he could not afford the high fees for treatment and costs of medication. Additionally, he was an illegal immigrant and could not access health care benefits. 'Sometimes I am happy and then suddenly I feel sad and suicidal. I do not know about these feelings.'

Vladimir nodded. He felt he understood this mental state. 'You could be paranoid schizophrenic like me. I am using some tablets and could give you some until you are cured.' He looked over his shoulder and saw a man watching him. He checked his pocket and found a crumpled piece of paper. It was a list of nine items. He was supposed to visit Staples.

Jose was overjoyed. 'I will be glad to use it, once it is not illegal like cocaine or meth because that will get me in jail.'

Vladimir laughed. It appeared as a confident laugh but he was afraid. 'No, of course it is not illegal. These were prescribed by my pharmacist. Also you need to watch cartoons and the Comedy Channel. Learn to love life and laugh more.' He paused and had a serious expression. 'Listen, don't turn around quickly but I believe the man seated near Terminal 3 is a U.S. agent who has been hunting me down for two years.'

Jose checked but there was nobody who fitted the description. 'Are you sure?'

'Look at the man in the blue suit and sunglasses.'

'Yes I see him.'

Vladimir began to panic. 'I believe he is after me because he thinks I am a Russian spy. I have seen similar scenes on the television series- Person of Interest. I have read about this in old newspapers like the Weekly World News. All this is true like stories on the existence of UFOs, conspiracy theories, abduction by extraterrestrials or that Elvis Presley is still alive. You have to see the movie Conspiracy Theory. These things make me suffer from paranoia and hysteria...I cannot trust anybody.'

Jose raised his eyebrows and began to sweat. 'Okay calm down. Have you been taking Prozac, Zoloft, Chantix or Ambien?' His nails were discoloured. There was a long scar on the left side of his face.

'Those sound familiar but I'm not sure of the names for these. Look, it's some green, blue and yellow tablets. One of these is some sort of anti-anxiety tablet and the others are antidepressants.' He slapped his chest and tapped his head. 'It is supposed to make me normal. Look I'm healthy, ordinary and normal.' He had a confused and frightened expression. His breathing was erratic.

'Look the man in the blue suit has boarded a flight!' said a relieved Jose. His heart rate increased and beads of sweat rolled down his temples. It was an adrenaline rush.

Vladimir was still convinced the man was a government agent. 'He will be back. I've seen a scene just like this in the movies- Enemy of the State and The 6th Day. It's a ploy to allow me to believe nobody is following me.' He became worried and glanced over his shoulder.

Jose bid him farewell and told him to go home and relax. He stopped at Wells Fargo to discuss a mortgage and then bought dinner at Taco Cabana.

The next day Vladimir gave fourteen tablets to Jose. 'This will last you for two weeks and then I will give you some more.' He sat on a bench and opened his lunch bowl and saw crawfish, friend catfish and oysters. It was leftovers from food purchased at Krab Kingz. In the evening he planned to get some movies from 24/7 Video and buy dinner at Olive Garden.

After five days, Vladimir and Jose met during their lunch-time. Vladimir dreaded the impending talk. He unwrapped his sandwich from Church's Chicken.

Jose was upbeat and positive, 'These tablets are amazing. I'm sleeping good, have a lot of energy and excited to come to work. Mabel would be arguing with me and this no longer bothers me. The children will be shouting and fighting and I am calm.' He checked his lunchbox. It was three tacos from El Rancho. He poured sauce on a taco and began eating. It was cold.

Vladimir recalled one of the advertisements on cable television and decided to warn him. 'These tablets are not for everyone. Talk to your doctor if you have high fever, confusion, high blood pressure, seizure, blurred vision, shortness of breath, bleeding gums, trouble swallowing, impaired judgment and dizziness.'

'Yeah okay.' It was not the advice Jose expected. He bit into another taco. 'Please I don't want to die here.' One hour later, he regained his composure and continued his work.

In the evening, Vladimir said goodbye to Jose and his friends. This was his last day at work. Next week he would begin a new job at the JFK Airport in New York. He and his family would be renting a three bedroom apartment on the sixth floor. Before arriving home, he stopped at Firearms and Ammo. His wife had given him a list of guns she wanted.

New York was hectic but Vladimir soon got accustomed. The apartment had a small porch. He opened the sliding door and stepped into the porch. He felt the evening wind blow through his hair. The pet hamster moved in its cage. It was hungry.

Sumintra was seated on the kitchen floor cutting coupons. She regularly boasted that she saved hundreds of dollars every month at the grocery. She had a scab on her left arm. This was due to a cut from broken glass which she received whilst digging in a dumpster searching for old newspapers. She asked neighbours and relatives for their old newspapers. Every morning before Vladimir departed for work she reminded him to check tables and seats for unwanted newspapers.

Each room in the apartment was slowly transformed into storage areas for products bought with coupons and food stamps. There were tins of Campbell's Chicken Soup under the four beds, the kitchen had Gillette razors, tins of sardines, packs of Chips Ahoy cookies, boxes of diapers and Pop-Tarts. Near the doorway was

Cadbury chocolates and Viva paper towels. In the kitchen were two refrigerators and a freezer filled with expired milk, hot dogs, frozen pizzas, bottles of orange juice, chicken, hamburger patties, containers of eggs, cheese and strawberries.

In the living room there were bars of soap, bottles of Kraft Salad Dressing, packs of Orbit Gum, forty bottles of Shout, eighty boxes of Tylenol, eleven boxes of Cracker Jack, a loaf of bread, fifteen bottles of ketchup, sixty bottles of shampoo and various brands of dental floss. The food items were behind the television, scattered on the ground and under two couches. The bathroom had carrots, macaroni, one hundred bottles of dishwashing liquid, eight large bags of rice and miscellaneous bottles of seasoning. The porch was impassable due to cases of Dr. Pepper, Pepsi, Sprite and Coca-Cola. And, packs of Oral-B toothbrushes, bottles of mayonnaise, Voortum Cookies, cans of Lady Speed Stick deodorant, combs, rolls of toilet paper, large bags of Purina dog chow and nine dented cans of Friskies Dry Cat Food.

Sumintra felt that she could be more effective in cutting her monthly household budget. She read Stephen Covey's Seven Habits of Highly Effective People, attended seminars and watched motivational videos. She carefully placed coupons in separate, labeled folders. After cutting coupons, she would give the newspapers to Jose who enjoyed reading the outdated news. Both had furniture and clothing in a rented section of the nearby Public Storage.

One Friday evening, she spent six hours buying five items in The Food Emporium located on 49th Street and 8th Avenue. She slowly read labels of products, compared in-store deals and double-checked prices. She also spent considerable time seeking advice from aisle attendants and other shoppers. She placed a 12-pack of German beer and two packs of salmon fillet in her cart. She was hungry and wanted to buy a muffin but decided it was not economical because she did not have a coupon for a discount. Ten minutes later she decided the salmon was too expensive and returned both packs to the frozen food section. She placed two bags of dog food in her cart and moved to the next aisle. She stopped and checked her coupons and took eight bottles of Beech Nut Baby Food, two packs of baby diapers, two bags of Purina Puppy Chow, seventeen cans of Friskies Dry Cat Food and two bags of Hartz Cat Litter. She stared at a bottle of 7-Up and remembered that last week she had purchased three soft drinks. After twenty minutes of indecision she finally decided to get the bottle of 7-Up. She hurried to the shelf, grabbed the bottle and headed for a cashier. She opened her purse and gave him coupons, food stamps and the Bonus Savings Club card.

'Good evening marm.' The cashier smiled and glanced at the items in the cart. 'So how are your pets and babies?' He swiped the card and returned it to her. His shirt was oversized and crumpled. There was a toothpaste stain on his shirt.

'Oh, the babies and dogs and cats are fine. Just buying the usual food for them.'

'You must enter them in our Pet Contest next month.'

She nodded. She had coupons to get fifty cents off Blue Diamond Almonds, one dollar off Sun-Maid Raisins and sixty cents off each bottle of Comet.

He checked the coupons and food stamps and passed a hand-held electronic device over the bar codes. The machine beeped and the cashier smiled. 'That will be $9.74 marm.' He was a middle-aged migrant from Iran. He had a noticeable paunch and flabby arms. Two months ago, he was a victim of racial profiling. This was his second job. His wife was three months pregnant and his two sons were in high school.

She expected a lower price and reluctantly gave him ten dollars. She waited for the change and receipt. Before entering the subway station she again counted the coins to ensure the cashier did not make an error. After exiting the station she purchased a chicken sandwich at a newly opened deli. She complained that the sandwich was too expensive and demanded a discount. The food attendant smiled and did not reply.

Sumintra exited and hurried to her home. She quietly entered the kitchen and hurriedly ate the sandwich. This was a common trait because she did not want to share food with other family members.

Next day, Vladimir was in the kitchen. He had a bowl and container of milk on the table. He opened and closed cupboards. 'Dear do we have any cornflakes or Quaker Oats?'

She was using a hairdryer and did not hear him. He banged on the door and repeated the question.

'Not sure. Check in de porch or living room.'

He cursed and slowly headed for the living room. He checked under the couches, behind the television and then went to the porch. He moved the food items hoping to find cornflakes or oats. 'No I'm not seeing any. Did you buy any Trix, Total, Frosted Flakes, Sugar Crisp or Cheerios recently?' He remembered the cornflakes that he ate when he was younger- Sugar Smacks, Ranger Joe, Cocoa Puffs, Fruit Loops and Sugar Pops.

She shouted, 'Check in the bathroom for a box of Wheaties, Rice Krispies, Banana Nut Crunch, Corn Pops, Cap'n Crunch, Special K. If you don't find any, try some Cracker Jack. I think I bought some last week at Walmart.'

He then decided on a tuna sandwich. He liked Starkist Solid White Tuna in oil. However, he realized there was no tuna and could not find the can opener. He went to the porch and saw recent purchases- two large bags of Kibbles n'Bits and three bags of Purina Pro Plan and Beneful. He checked to see if the neighbours were watching and reluctantly opened one of the bags. He took two handfuls, smelled it and then carefully placed it in a bowl with milk. He slowly stirred it with a wooden spoon. His arm was trembling as he placed a spoonful in his mouth and began chewing. He felt nauseous and swallowed. He suddenly realized the taste was agreeable and had another spoonful of puppy chow and milk. It was crunchy and reminded him of cornflakes. He also enjoyed the dog snacks- Meaty Bone and Scooby Snacks. These were cheaper than the Doritos, Cheetos and Pringles that his family enjoyed.

During the next month, for breakfast, he would have dog food and milk. His friends felt his hair looked glossy and shiny. And, he no longer suffered from constipation. He read the ingredients of Purina Beneful and saw it had 'real beef and wholesome grains' and Purina Pro Plan had 'wholesome rice and high levels of antioxidants.' He felt this was nutritious and quietly encouraged his two children to eat the dog food and dog snacks. It seemed to have a positive effect on Ali who no longer needed Ritalin. Both kids stopped their special vitamins- Lil Critters Gummy Vites.

One evening, Vladimir agreed to prepare dinner. He boiled pasta and opened a can of mixed vegetables. He searched for tinned tuna or salmon but realized there was none in the apartment. He was frustrated and annoyed and wanted to dump the pasta. He saw two tins of Friskies and a bag of Catnip. He read the ingredients and shook his head. Friskies had thirty vitamins and minerals and was supposed to have 'high quality protein for growing muscles.' It seemed healthier than the sausages which he enjoyed. After twenty minutes he decided to open two tins of cat food and added it to the pasta. 'Nikki come and set the table.'

Nikita entered the kitchen and opened packages of plastic spoons, paper cups and plates. To avoid the task of buying and washing dishes and cutlery, her lazy mother bought disposable cups, plates and spoons.

The entire family enjoyed the meal. Sumintra licked her lips. 'This is a great meal. One of the best you ever made!'

'Yes dad, it tastes like you added some exotic spice,' said Nikita.

Ali added, 'Yes, compliments to the chef! Daddy you are a great cook.'

Vladimir smiled but was angry that the apartment was stocked with items that they did not need. He sternly said to his wife, 'Listen, I said it before but you need to buy food and items we need. Look how much dog food, baby food and cat food we have!'

'What wrong with dat?' asked Sumintra.

'We don't have a cat or dog! We have no pets! And we don't have any babies!'

This did not bother her. 'But we can buy a cat and a dog. I suppose we can adopt a baby.'

'Adopt a baby? Honey you cannot even care for the children we have and you want to adopt! Look last week the hamster almost died of starvation,' her husband continued, 'cut down on the time you spend on cutting coupons and help with the children's homework. Go and pay some of the bills. Look AT&T disconnected us because we did not pay.' He stared at the two tattoos on her arm- a rose and her name. He never understood why persons would want to have their names tattooed on themselves.

'Mummy, listen to daddy he is right,' said Nikita, 'look we have no fabric softener, ketchup, salt and foil paper. The cable bill has been unpaid for four months.'

Vladimir continued, 'And you need to slow down on buying. I usually get sick from drinking milk that is expired. Use those food stamps wisely. And I feel claustrophobic amidst all this food lying around the rooms. The eggs are discolored and look as if they are ready for hatching.'

Sumintra smiled and casually dismissed their concerns, 'You always making jokes about stale or spoilt food. Okay I will make some changes around here and will monitor the use of the food stamps. Let's enjoy this delicious meal and give thanks that we have food. Think of all the starving, poor, skinny children in Africa and India who cannot get a decent meal like this.' She continued eating and avoided eye contact with her children and husband. The rest of the family remained quiet. They doubted that positive changes would occur.

Next morning, Vladimir began making sandwiches for lunch. The sandwiches comprised mayonnaise, chopped celery, garlic and cat food. He found these sandwiches were tastier than the hot dogs and cheese sandwiches. For dessert he would have a small bottle of Gerber's baby food. A routine annual blood test revealed reductions in cholesterol and blood pressure. This made him believe that the cat, baby and dog foods were responsible for his improved health. He did not mention this to his wife because he felt she would buy more of these foods. On Fridays, he shared the cat food sandwiches with Jose.

Cockroaches and rats began attacking some of the foodstuffs that were stored in the apartment. Sumintra decided to use some of the coupons to buy bug sprays, rat bait and cockroach traps. She also gave some of the traps to Jose who also had problems with cockroaches at work.

She visited Food Plus supermarket in Queens. It had West Indian foods and she bought a container of aloe juice. She laughed when she saw a carton of goat milk and a can with callaloo. She was accustomed obtaining fresh goat's milk and callaloo in the Caribbean. Two shelves were lined with different varieties of pepper sauce. She chose Red Rooster hot sauce. There were trays with mangoes and each one had a small sticker that said- 'Hecho en Mexico.' Nearby trays had bananas from Yucatan and the avocadoes were from Guatemala. She did not buy these fruits because she felt the prices were too high. She rarely went to West Indian supermarkets because there were few discounts and no coupons for the items she wanted. They also seemed small and crowded.

The cashiers at Food Emporium were accustomed to her antics and her thick folders with coupons. Trips to the grocery needed careful planning and were tiring but she felt victorious. She felt more of her time should be devoted to couponing. During the subway ride to her home, she always considered resigning from her job and spending more time collecting newspapers, cutting coupons and shopping.

She frequently discussed the idea with her husband but he did not approve. His replies were usually consistent. 'Why? We have enough groceries to last us for two years! We don't need any more food items. We need two salaries to help pay the rent.'

She shook her head. 'My job is boring and I receive little pay. It would be better for our budget if I stay home and focus more on cutting coupons. We have to be more economical.' She pointed to a 6-pack of Cottonelle Double Roll Bath Tissue. 'I got those for fifty cents and this was because I had my coupons. But I could have gotten six of these paper towels for FREE if I had more coupons. I got one dollar off the salad dressing but could have gotten a discount of four dollars if I had more coupons. I wanted to buy canned vegetables and canned tomatoes but I had no coupons.'

He realized that she would not change her mind. 'Okay, go ahead and do what you feel is best.' He took a mouthful of Honey Nut Cheerios.

That evening she submitted her resignation letter. She stopped to buy ten Powerball lottery tickets. She saw homeless persons on the sidewalk sleeping on old newspapers. Some of the homeless persons used newspapers to stuff their clothes to keep warm during the nights. She desperately wanted the coupons from these papers. She patiently waited for three hours until they fell asleep and then stole their newspapers.

She crossed the street and entered a small ethnic grocery. It was brightly lit and there were colourful signs. She went to the back of the grocery and began browsing the shelves. She found a shelf with soft and damaged fruits and vegetables, expired drinks and stale pastries. She checked the price of the package with three rotten kiwis. It was sixty cents. She smiled and felt this was a great deal. She carefully placed two packs in her cart and then selected a soft cantaloupe, two packages of bruised strawberries and deformed blueberries and three sickly-looking apples with scrapes and black spots. Packs of black carrots, damaged pears and soft peppers also went into her cart. Her final selections were stale Kaiser dinner rolls and expired yogurt. Every night she would check websites such as couponsuzy.com to check the latest discounts and then she would use a calculator to check that her receipts from the grocery were accurate.

She wanted to eliminate money being spent on cologne, mouthwash and deodorants because she felt these items were too expensive.

Vladimir carefully unwrapped the sandwich from Dennys. He licked his lips and closed his eyes. It had cheddar cheese, crispy bacon and eggs. The other package had pancakes for the children. He gave them their food.

That evening, she had a frank discussion with her husband and children. 'Instead of using deodorants and colognes, it would be much more economical if we spray our bodies or clothes with air freshener.'

Their dinner comprised Cinnamon Toast Crunch and Lucky Charms. Her husband stopped eating and began to laugh. 'You joking, right? You not serious? We now living worse than rednecks,' he mumbled.

'But mummy nobody else does do that,' said Ali, 'even poor people does use deodorant. Why we cannot use it?' He was dismayed and poured syrup on his pancake.

She had a stern look, 'Ali stop being rude and eat your pancake. Only geniuses like myself are able to think of these ideas to cut costs. I am a Financial Consultant.' She paused. 'In fact, I'm better, I'm a coach…yes a money coach. We have to save money, I want to carry the children to Disneyland. The air fresheners have a nice smell.' She briefly left the room and returned with two bottles of Febreze. 'Look I am able to get these two bottles for less than five dollars because of my coupons.' Ali was sad. He ran to the living room and sat on the couch. His sister was watching his favorite show, Here Comes Honey Boo Boo. Ali left and returned with a bowl of Golden Grahams and milk.

Next day Nikita returned home and proudly said, 'Mummy, my friends at school saying I smelling like fresh flowers.'

'See I told you it would be nice, you remind them of Spring,' said Sumintra. She opened a bottle of Mr. Clean and sniffed it. 'Hmmm what a nice lavender scent.' She poured some in a bucket of water and began to mop. 'I'm also going to cut down on the money we spend on desserts. No more money on chocolates, ice-cream and cake. These are also not healthy, too much sugar and saturated fats.'

'What will we have?' asked Nikita.

'I've noticed that snacks for dogs are cheaper. We are going to start eating Dingo Roos, Munchy Stix and Smokehouse Lamb bone, knee bone and rib bone.' Sumintra stopped mopping. 'The water bill is too high. We need to cut down on flushing the toilet and washing wares. I think we should forever use disposable plates.'

Nikita and Ali grimaced. Vladimir smiled. 'So how will we reduce flushing toilets?' He knew this madness would never end.

'I am glad you asked. The children will have to pee outside and also will have to bury their shit in the yard.'

'No mummy I don't want to poop outside like an animal,' said Nikita.

'Yeah right.' Vladimir wanted to change the topic. 'So tell me about the beaches in the Caribbean. What time do the beaches close?'

Sumintra laughed. 'Close? Love, beaches don't close dey open all the time.'

Nikita and Ali laughed.

He felt insulted. 'Why do you always buy so much food and drinks?'

His wife replied, ‘The world will end soon, the Mayan calendar say so. If not, we have to be ready for the comet that will hit Earth or the Zombie Apocalypse which can occur anytime. We need to buy lots more guns and bullets and grenades to kill the zombies. We need to have lots more food in storage so we wouldn’t have to go outside to face the zombies.’ Both children became afraid.

Vladimir moaned. He wanted to be away from home and decided to spend the next four days travelling to various states. He visited the San Diego Museum of Art, the High Museum of Art in Georgia and the Corcoran Gallery of Art in Washington D.C. He liked the Museum of Russian Icons and the Norman Rockwell Museum in Massachusetts. He enjoyed being on the trains and buses. After his exhausting trip, he returned home and spent most of the night arguing with his wife about clipping coupons. He went into the bedroom and switched on the television. He watched episodes of Card Sharks and Who wants to be a Millionaire then fell asleep.

Sumintra criticized his recent visits. ‘All this travelling was a waste of money. Why not view art right here in the Guggenheim Museum, de Brooklyn Museum of Art, New Museum of Contemporary Art, Metropolitan Museum of Art or de Children’s Museum in Manhattan?’

‘But I’ve been to most of those places many times.’

‘I’m trying to save money and you are wasting it.’ She felt this was a major depressive episode and rushed to the medicine cabinet. She opened vials and took Lexapro, Paxil and Effexor. Three days later, she decided to relax by visiting the Central Park Zoo and attend a musical performance at Carnegie Hall. Upon returning home she felt a sense of relief. It was a much needed break from the monotony of arguments, cutting coupons and buying groceries. One month later she still felt the need to visit other sites. She went to the New York Aquarium in Coney Island, the Prospect Park Zoo in Brooklyn. She attended ballets at the Dance Theatre of Harlem and listened to opera, jazz and the New York Philharmonic at the Lincoln Center for Performing Arts. She enjoyed the singing of Le Nozze di Figaro, an Italian, and Eugene Onegin, a Russian. Her husband reluctantly accompanied her to the performance of War and Peace by the Metropolitan Opera. For the first time she heard Beethoven’s Symphony No. 2 in D major. After the event, she stopped at Walgreens and purchased Panadol tablets.

That night whilst on the subway, she wished her life was more exciting. She decided that it would be good to be part of the audience in the live airing of Jerry Springer, Bill Cunningham Show, Dr. Oz, The View, Rachael Ray, Oprah, Richie, The Wendy Williams Show, The Doctors, Judge Mathis, Dr. Phil and Judge Judy. It was expensive to travel across the United States but she enjoyed being part of the live audience and felt glad when friends said they briefly spotted her on television.

Ali complained to his father, 'I don't like using these air fresheners. Mummy only buying two scents- wild berries and honey or white orchid and bloom. I rather not use anything. Also, it making my skin itch.'

Vladimir frowned. 'The damn air fresheners gave me a rash. When she returns tomorrow I will try to convince her to allow us to use deodorants and perfumes.' He wished that he had never met and married Sumintra.

For Christmas Day, Sumintra gave her husband and children small packs of Hershey Valentine Kisses. These milk chocolates cost US$2.79 per pack and were rancid because she had purchased them in February on Valentine's Day. Vladimir was disappointed to receive his present because he spent considerable money to buy her a large stuffed Perugina Baci Bear, a silver necklace and an expensive box of Maison de Belgium Chocolate seashells. The children gave their mother a blood pressure kit, as a gift.

In 2002, the miserly Sumintra filed for divorce. She felt her lifestyle was not compatible with Vladimir. It was neither a prolonged nor messy divorce. He asked to keep the apartment and she agreed. She wanted the groceries in all the rooms. She did not want to keep the children as this would mean additional expenses. He willingly agreed to have full custody of both children who attained full status under the new law- Deferred Action for Childhood Arrivals. The United States Immigration and Customs Enforcement had been searching for Sumintra. They wanted to deport her to Guyana.

Chapter 3
Talented and gifted

When Ali was twenty years he decided to leave his father's apartment. It was because the apartment was very cluttered and he had to pay a weekly rent to his father. He moved into a nearby apartment building on 8th Avenue in New York. Despite disapproval from his parents, he married Indeerah who was an illegal immigrant from India. She was a temporary clerk at a store in the nearby mall. She was a vegetarian and non-smoker. She ate foods that were fresh and disliked fried and oily foods and drinks that had preservatives and coloring. She was tall, slim, had short hair, fair-skinned and had fifteen tattoos on her neck, arms and legs. She had tattoos of two angels, a butterfly, two cobra snakes, spiders, monkeys and a dog.

Ali worked as a bus driver for the NYCTA on the M27 line. After two years he was fired because he was always late for the job and complained of being unable to fit into the driver's seat. He tipped the scales at seven hundred and ten pounds and this obesity contributed to health problems. He received a disability allowance and this allowed him to pay his monthly rent and food bills. He obtained legal advice and decided to sue the New York Bus Corporation for not providing larger seats and more room between the steering wheel and driver. His lawyers argued this was discrimination against overweight ethnic minorities. He received $4 million in compensation. He used some of this money to purchase a home in Rochester.

On mornings, at 8am, a typical breakfast comprised nine fried eggs, four slices of toasted bread, bacon, three slices of cake, a large bowl of Fruity Pebbles cornflakes, two glasses of chocolate milk and a box of Pop-Tarts. At 10am he would have a snack comprising five packs of vanilla pudding, a tall glass of Coca-Cola and a large bowl of vanilla or strawberry ice-cream. For lunch, the layout consisted of fried chicken wings, mashed potatoes, four slices of pizza, three burritos, two cans of Dr. Pepper and a hamburger. At 5pm, he had an evening snack of three milkshakes, a plate of chocolate chip cookies and five hotdogs. His dinner at was usually fries, chicken nuggets, curried shrimps and five cans of Budweiser beer.

Seven months after leaving his job, he tipped the scales at eight hundred pounds and could not leave his room. For two years the room became his prison. He had five tattoos on his chest depicting a hamburger, packet of fries, hot-dog, pizza and a box of fried chicken. On his left arm he had a tattoo of a Sprite bottle and on his right arm there was a tattoo of a Pepsi bottle.

He was confined to his bed because his legs could not support his bulky frame. He could not fit into the toilet and shower. His wife prepared his daily meals, gave him a weekly bath and regularly emptied his bedpan. She gave him two insulin tablets after each meal and also administered other medications including Lovaza, Livalo, Crestor and Lipitor. She always ignored the expiry dates on the medicines because she felt terrible to discard medicines.

Ali spent each day sleeping, eating and watching television. He enjoyed reruns of Bad Girls Club, Cheaters, King of Queens, Big Brother, Baywatch, Paradise Hotel, Millionaire Matchmaker, Fear Factor, The Bachelor, Rock of Love and A Shot of Love. Every day he watched two hours of the Food Channel and eagerly followed the soap operas- Bold and Beautiful, General Hospital and The Young and the Restless, As the World Turns, Days of our Lives, All My Children and One Life to Live. He said aloud, 'All these soap operas have a sort of musical bed occurring. He also viewed reruns of Dallas, Knots Landing, Dynasty, Falcon Crest and Peyton Place. He knew the times of each show and often had the latest copy copy of Soap Opera Digest on his lap.

On Valentine's Day, Ali wanted to do something romantic for his wife. After devouring his lunch he took the chicken bones and three fries and made a heart-shaped formation on his plate. He then blew a kiss for her.

She forced a smile. She was agitated and felt pity for this pathetic life form who was confined to a room. She went into the kitchen and placed water in a pan that was on the stove. She lit the stove and opened a cupboard. There was a bottle of Folgers coffee. After drinking the coffee she placed the cup among the growing heap of dirty dishes in the sink. She dressed and went to purchase food.

She entered a deli and bought containers of Caprese salad, Mediterranean pasta salad, rice pudding, tofu and Swiss cheese. It was raining and she decided to buy a cup of tea and sit at a table. One hour later she returned home and emptied the groceries.

Ali shouted, 'Did you buy cheesecake and chocolate mousse?'

'No.'

He was enraged. 'What the hell!! What about bologna, pork chops and steak? There is no damn cornflakes in the house! Did you buy Cocoa Pebbles?' He took a mouthful of Bud Light.

'No, I went to buy some items for myself.' She opened a carton of milk.

He began to sob. 'Why are you neglecting me? Don't you love me? It's Valentine's Day. I feel so unloved.' He touched his forehead and grimaced. 'All this stress is the cause for my gastric ulcers and migraines.'

She was exasperated. She entered his room and stared at him in disbelief.

'This attitude makes me depressed and when I am depressed I eat a lot.' He wiped the tears trickling down his fat cheeks and avoided her gaze. He threw the beer can on the ground and stuck his fingers in a large bag of Frito Lay's Dorito Chips. After the bag was empty he crumpled it and angrily threw it on the ground. He then gobbled up a dozen Pepperidge Farm Milano Cookies and two packs of Utz potato chips and pretzels. 'I want to run for president.' He looked at her reaction. He stuck his hand in a pack of M&M's and grabbed a handful.

She casually remarked, 'President of what? The neighborhood watch group or of this house?'

'Those type of comments make me feel suicidal. I want to be the president of the USA.'

She twisted her mouth and then stared at him. 'Really? Are you serious? Who will vote for you? Who will provide huge donations?'

He coughed. 'Yes, I am serious. The fast food restaurants will provide financial help or else I will threaten to sue them.' He placed a Slinky on his forehead and allowed it to slowly move to his chest and belly.

She looked at the toy gliding over his large frame. 'Do you think the Americans will take you serious? Which party will endorse you- Democrats or Republicans?'

'I will form my own party. Now is the time for a new party in American politics. A new way of thinking.' He began chewing on a Twizzler. 'The obese people of this great country will vote for me. You see I've realized that obese people are everywhere. Both men and women are fat. In all religions, classes and ethnic groups there is a high level of fatness. Fat people are people too. Fat people must be treated like people.' He began to breathe heavily and clutched his chest. 'I'm having some pains. Do you think we should call an ambulance?'

'No, it could be some indigestion or gas, here take some aspirin.' She quickly opened a drawer and took two aspirins, that had passed the expiry dates, and placed them in his mouth. He had crumbs and pieces of chicken skin on his chest and belly. He swallowed the aspirins. She switched channels. There was an episode of Real Housewives of New York City.

He shouted at the television screen, 'You are a fool to leave your man!' A few minutes later he screamed, 'What an idiot! How women could think that way.' After the show ended he viewed The Moment of Truth, Manson Girls, Entertainment Tonight and Showbiz Tonight.

'Honey please be calm,' she pleaded.

He continued to shout and curse at the television. This was a habit that his wife hated.

At 11pm, after a short nap he realized the chest pain was no longer there, 'I'm feeling to eat something different like Chinese food. Get some!'

'It's late. You should not be eating so late. It's not healthy,' said Indeerah. She was tired.

He pouted. 'I really feel unloved. You also promised to carry me to visit Disneyland, Hollywood and Disney World but never did. You promised to take me to the West Coast to buy burgers at In-N-Out but you never did.'

She was exasperated and nodded. 'Okay I'll order some food for us. I didn't forget, I am saving money for those trips.' Nearby was a pile of sixteen telephone books and outdated television guides. She checked the most recent issue of the telephone book and found China Star located on 8th Avenue. The restaurant offered free delivery. She called and placed the dinner order.

Whilst waiting, he ate nine packs of Skittles and eight Twinkies. His dinner arrived and comprised crispy sesame beef, lemon chicken, moo shu pork, sautéed bean sprouts, beef in garlic sauce, egg drop soup, pork dumplings, fried scallops, Cantonese noodles, tai chien chicken, squid in black bean sauce, prawns in chili sauce, lobster in garlic sauce and roast duck. After the meal, Indeera carefully washed the Styrofoam food containers and placed them in a cupboard which contained empty bottles and dirty dishes. Her dinner was a glass of green tea and sandwich with whole wheat bread, grated Parmesan cheese and fresh basil leaves.

Two hours later, Ali shouted, 'I am hungry, order some damn pizzas.'

'Okay.' She was angry that her sleep was disturbed but did not want to argue. She checked Domino's Pizza and ordered two large Extravangzza pizzas with a variety of toppings- ground beef, black olives, extra mozzarella cheese, pepperoni, ham, sausage, mushrooms and onions.

Five minutes later he shouted, 'Don't forget to order the damn side orders and dessert. Maybe order an extra pizza for tomorrow. You forgot to do it last week and I almost starved to death!' He focused on the television series Wife Swap. He looked at his wife and wished he could swap her for someone who could cook or feed him lots of food.

She called and placed the additional order for Domino's Mexican Sizzler, chicken wings, potato wedges, coleslaw, waffles, chocolate chip cookies and Häagen-dazs ice cream. After the meal, she gave him a dosage of insulin. 'So what causes you to eat so much?'

Ali sighed. 'Well to tell you the truth, when I was younger my mother caused my pet hamster to die. She did not want us to buy pet food for it. It was very traumatic.' He began to cry. 'As a teenager I suffered more trauma. I badly wanted to join a circus but was rejected because I was too thin.' He continued to cry and his wife consoled him until he stopped crying. The doorbell rang. He asked in a frightened voice, 'Are you expecting anyone?'

She shook her head.

He thought for awhile and said, 'Maybe is Mabel who promised to come and give me some counseling.'

Indeerah went to the door and checked. It was Mabel. She opened the door and smiled. 'Welcome, we have been expecting you. Come right in and follow me.' Mabel frowned when she saw the messy house. She entered Ali's room and was surprised to see his size.

'Hello, glad you could make it,' said Ali. He was eating a large pizza from Little Caesars.

Mabel sat on a chair and began writing in a notepad.

'Have we started the counseling session?' asked Ali.

Mabel nodded. 'Hmm, yes I'm making some preliminary notes on your mood. So tell me when do you get angry? Are you constipated? Do you get headaches? Do you see ghosts?'

'I am angry whenever I am hungry. I'm also angry when I want to see a show on television. I don't believe in ghosts and get headaches after watching more than twelve hours of television each day.'

Mabel wrote five sentences in her notepad. 'When are you sad?'

'Whenever someone dies in a television show or movie I feel really sad and often cry. I guess I'm just an emotional teddy bear.'

'Do you get suicidal thoughts?' asked Mabel. She continued writing.

Ali was pensive and then replied, 'Yes, whenever I am hungry and also a few times when a show is cancelled or if a food place is closed. But luckily I cannot move to the kitchen to get a knife. Also, I was refused a credit card by a bank so I cannot buy a gun over the telephone…so it's difficult for me to get something to commit suicide but I want to. So you see being this large size is a blessing in disguise.'

Mabel shook her head and continued. 'When do you feel embarrassed?'

'I use to feel ashamed that I could not use the toilet or bathe like normal people, but now I am accustomed to my lifestyle of bathing with a sponge and pail. My wife has to help me bathe because I am helpless.'

She turned a page and continued writing. 'Are you happy in your marriage?'

He lowered his voice. 'Whenever there is food in this house I feel my marriage is blessed. When I am hungry I feel like getting a divorce….' He paused because Indeerah walked into the room. 'Bring me some cereal, I am hungry. All this talking make me get really hungry.'

Indeerah nodded and exited the room.

Mabel continued scribbling in her notepad. She excitedly shouted, 'I've finally made a diagnosis of you!'

His wife returned with two large bowls of Apple Jacks and Raisin Bran and placed them on his lap. Some milk spilled on his knee. She remained in the room.

Ali was not amused. 'Really?'

'What is it?' asked Indeerah.

Mabel was stern. 'You are polypolar. It's a rare condition and actually you are the first person I have seen displaying symptoms. Also you are suffering from Binge-eating disorder.' She adjusted her spectacles.

Indeerah was agitated and annoyed upon hearing Mabel's diagnosis. 'What does it mean?'

She opened a book and slowly turned the pages. The book was titled Diagnostic and Statistical Manual of Mental Diseases. 'Ali suffers from a schizoaffective disorder. Also, he could be displaying fear, anger, apathy, hate, happiness, sadness and embarrassment at the same time or in a short space of time. He is a talented and gifted man.'

Ali looked at Indeerah and said, 'You see, I am special and need to be treated with care and love. Bring me two boxes of Rice Krispies.'

Indeerah nodded. She gave four hundred dollars to Mabel. This was a special fee which included a house visit.

Three times each week, in the night, Indeerah would quietly take the neighbours' garbage bags to her garage. She would place the bags on a table and empty each one. Then she would spend two hours checking the contents of the bags. She was curious and wanted to know what her neighbours were eating and drinking. Sometimes she found partially eaten and expired foods and these were put aside for Ali. She was excited whenever she found broken toys and household items. These would be kept in her backyard. After she would tie the bags and return them to her neighbours' bins.

One morning after a large breakfast, Ali complained that the tightness in his chest had returned. He was sweating. 'I'm having some problems breathing. You should dial 911.' He grimaced.

Indeerah calmly responded. 'It's just indigestion again. Remember you suffer from reflux. It will soon go away.' She poured some Pepto Bismol in a glass of water. The glass was dirty. 'Here try this. If it does not work I'll get something else.'

He reluctantly drank it. After one hour the pain did not subside and Indeerah gave him Prevacid, Alka-Seltzer, Pepcid and Tums. All had passed their expiry dates. After the pain subsided he had his morning snack whilst watching episodes of CSI Miami, Harlem Heights, Futurama and Candy Girls. He had lunch during the airing of Toddlers &Tiaras, America's Prom Queen and I Know my Kid's a Star. He sighed and said, 'I should think about having some children.'

She frowned. She wanted to maintain the platonic relationship and dreaded the idea of bearing his children. 'Yes dear I would like that. Maybe next year.' She changed channels. 'Let's watch this program.' It was Beyond Scared Straight on the A&E Channel. She took the Lysol container and sprayed it upwards.

He sneezed then shouted at the television program, 'What shit is this? I cannot believe that Americans watch this garbage. Only a complete idiot would like this.'

'Honey lemme change the channel,' said Indeerah. She adjusted her blouse. 'What you want to see? Scooby doo or Flintstones?'

'No leave it here. I want to see Beyond Scared Straight.' An hour later, he watched the Video Music Awards and laughed at the eccentric outfits worn by artistes. He laughed when he heard their childish statements when they received awards. He felt ashamed to be an American. 'I cannot believe these low standards are being accepted as normal. Imagine millions of people seeing this. I guess the artistes look weird and speak that way to attract fans. It is all a publicity stunt.' He looked at his wife, 'Is today Friday?'

She glanced at the calendar. 'No, it's Thursday.'

'Damn. I really wish it was Friday or Monday so I could see some wrestling.' He became depressed and began crying. Ten minutes later he began sneezing. 'It's all this dust in the room. You need to wash the curtains.' The room had crooked piles of old magazines, shelves with torn children's story books and rusty trophies. Strands of cobwebs and patches of mildew were on the ceiling. On the floor were stuffed toys, a broken tricycle, twenty outdated television guides, six non-functioning remote controls, empty medicine vials, empty and twisted beer cans and board games. He took Nasorex, Symbicort, Advil, Claritin, Zyrtec, Tamiflu, Piriton and Triz. The sneezing stopped after two hours. His mood changed and he became warm and friendly. The cocktail of medicines resulted in an allergic reaction and his wife ran for the EpiPen and administered a dosage. The incident made him drowsy and he slept for nine hours.

In the evening Indeerah washed the two curtains in his room. She sprayed more Lysol and felt this was important for a healthy home. She read the words on the container - 'Kills cold and flu virus.' She entered his room and saw him asleep. She laughed as she recalled his earlier suggestion of having children.

He awoke and shouted, 'Bring some food quick! I am starving! And I just had a dream that I was eating a plate of macaroni with lots of cheese. I'm feeling to eat some cake. Do we have any?'

She checked the fridge. 'No, we don't have no cake. I will bake a Betty Crocker cake and also call a restaurant and order some chicken nuggets, macaroni pie and fries.' She checked the calendar in the kitchen. 'Remember that Mabel coming here in ten minutes for your final session.'

Mabel soon arrived and rang the doorbell. She greeting Indeerah and cautiously walked to Ali's room. 'Good evening sir. How are you today?'

Ali forced a smile. 'I am okay, just a little hungry and thirsty.'

Mabel moved two empty KFC boxes from a chair and placed them on the floor. 'Yes, I could imagine.' The chair had mildew. She frowned and sat on the dirty, shaky chair. She began writing in her notebook. She waited for him to switch off the television. 'Please turn off the tv. So today we are going to talk about your sexuality.'

Ali switched off the television. The room had a strange silence and he felt uncomfortable.

Mabel asked him twenty questions but he responded to only two questions. After ten minutes she said, 'Hmm. That's interesting. I believe you are multi-gender or polygender.'

'What the hell is that?' he asked, 'do I have long to live and am I going to die?'

She calmly responded, 'It's a new sexuality that recently emerged.'

He and his wife had worried expressions.

'I am a Christian and don't think it's good for your soul…but let me be professional, I'm a trained psychotherapist and believe your problem is also psychosomatic. Your responses also indicate you have an identity crisis and also manic episodes.'

Indeerah seemed confused and asked, 'What type of shops sell food for these types of people? Where could I get furniture for polygender people? What type of car insurance do polygender have? What type of movies do polygender persons watch? What airlines do these type of persons use when flying? What drinks should polygender have? Would this make him creative?'

Mabel shook her head. 'I don't know, stop with all these difficult questions! You will have to check the internet.' She was irritated. 'And, stop calling them these people….I'm only trained to identify neuroses and psychoses in my patients.' She glanced at her wristwatch.

Ali profusely thanked her for the diagnosis. Indeerah reluctantly paid her two thousand dollars. Mabel signed the insurance form and next to her name wrote 'it/him/us/her/them'. She felt a sense of accomplishment and guaranteed that the sessions would improve Ali's life.

After Mabel departed, Ali became depressed and shouted for lots of food. He shoved six chicken nuggets in his mouth and began chewing. He quickly swallowed and grabbed more nuggets. He swallowed and then stuffed his mouth with fries but forgot to put ketchup and mustard on the fries. So he opened a bottle of Heinz Ketchup and packet of mustard and squeezed both into his mouth. He smiled as he chewed the nuggets and fries that were cooked in lard. He shouted at the television program, 'Come on fool drive faster to catch the damn bandit. Shoot him! Shoot him now!'

His wife scolded him, 'Stop shouting at the television. Stop eating like some animal in the jungle. Eat slowly and chew your food properly.' She looked at the steamed carrots, potatoes, parsley and cauliflower on her plate. She felt nauseous when she saw him eating meat.

Ali ignored her comments and continued chewing. He rammed a handful of fries into his mouth. He wiped his greasy fingers on the bed sheet. 'I think I need Blue Cross

Blueshield Insurance.' She did not reply. He switched the channel and saw part of Cheaters. 'Darling, would you ever cheat on me?'

She paused and touched the wedding ring on her finger. 'No dear, you are special to me.' She looked at the five trophies on the glass shelf near his chair. These were won by Ali in local eating competitions. Two years ago, he was banned from twelve restaurants which had 'All you can eat' and buffet specials.

'Yes, be grateful I'm not an alcoholic and also not guilty of domestic violence.' He bit into a drumstick and began eating cole slaw. He changed the channel and saw Iron Chef America. 'I've been thinking that maybe one day I will become famous as the fattest person in the world and have a wax figure of me in Madame Tussaud's Wax Museum. People from all over the world will come to see the wax statue. I will become an icon like Mother Teresa, Nelson Mandela or Gandhi.' He ate seventeen Klondike bars, five Pillsbury biscuits and a strawberry pie. The next show was Cupcake Wars. 'I'm not sure why but I'm feeling to eat cupcakes…lots of cupcakes.' He began to shove cole slaw into his mouth. Some fell on his chest. 'I'm still hungry, I wish you would give me more food portions.'

She ignored his comments and he continued to complain. The exasperated wife finally retorted, 'You stuff your face with food and then complain of pains and trouble breathing. Take your time and eat. The food is not running away. This is not a jungle or forest where other animals waiting to eat your food.' She used her knife and fork to cut the carrots and broccoli.

He wiped his mouth on a pillow and slowly reached for the remote control. He switched the station to National Geographic. There was a documentary on the Incas in South America. He checked Discovery Channel and saw an interview with terrorists. The next station- Animal Explorer had a documentary on lions hunting in Africa. He felt like a lion and began to roar. He felt like a king as he was in control of the room and the home.

'Let's watch LA Ink or NY Ink,' she said, 'I like those types of shows because it deals with tattoos. If it is not showing, let us watch Outsourced.'

Ali reluctantly agreed and pressed the remote until he found LA Ink. Next morning, after breakfast he said, 'For lunch we should order something different. I enjoyed the Chinese food we had recently.' He opened three packs of Reese's and emptied them in his mouth.

'But you ate so much and vomited.' Her breakfast was a vegetable burger consisting of sesame seeds, oregano, thyme, carrots, lettuce, cabbage, celery, mint and sage leaves. For lunch she had planned to buy soup, breadsticks and salad at Olive Garden. She constantly monitored her health using a portable Theranos blood analyzer. She left to wash her hands in the kitchen.

He shrugged. 'You worry too much, my body was not accustomed to Chinese food. For a long time I did not eat Chinese food. Let's try something exotic.' He was looking at a rerun of the Bachelor.

She returned to the room and dried her hands on a small towel. 'You mean toxic?' she murmured and rolled her eyes.

'I wish I was on a tv show like this so I could find somebody suitable.' He rubbed his belly. 'Hurry and bring more food, I'm hungry.'

She remembered seeing flyers for restaurants in the neighborhood. She went into the living room and checked the rack with mail. She found a flyer for Sargon which specialized in Vietnamese dishes. She ordered four main dishes and the side orders were fried rice with sausages and bean sprout and two Chow Fun noodle soups. He was angry that she did not order more food. He belched and closed his eyes. Soon he was snoring. After dinner she washed the chopsticks and placed them in a drawer that was filled with plastic spoons and forks. She kept the restaurant's brown bags and napkins in another drawer. On the kitchen floor were old syringes, empty medicine bottles, dirty baking pans, soiled foil paper and decaying fruit skins.

Next day, it was bleak and cold. It was Thanksgiving Day and Ali demanded a feast. He had slices of honey-cured ham, smoked turkey, buffalo-style chicken wings, lobster, crabs, all beef salami, pastrami, bologna and corned beef. After dinner, he drank an entire 18-pack Miller Lite Beer. For Christmas lunch, he had a 12-pack of Heineken, a rack of lamb and garlic beef rib roast with horseradish. And his dessert comprised carrot and cassata cakes, nine brownies, key lime pie, cheesecake, two pecan rings and four croissants.

On Ali's twenty-fifth birthday, he was 938 pounds. Sumintra ordered a double fudge chocolate cake and had it delivered to her son's home. He ate half of the cake during lunch. It reminded him of a cake he had seen on the television show- Cake Boss. Two days later, she sent him a bill and asked for compensation. He was confused and dialed his mother.

'Hello mum, what is this receipt of $25.80 for? Did you buy medicines?'

'Yes, that's the correct amount. It's for the cake and card I sent.'

He was confused. 'But I thought it was a birthday gift.'

'Dear, ever since the divorce, things have been hard for me. I'm finding it difficult to make ends meet. You should be glad that I remembered your birthday.'

He was angry. 'Please don't bother to give me gifts and cards for future birthdays and Christmas. I have a lot of debts. Send me a card or greeting via email. Look, I did not get anything from dad, see how nice he is.'

'Okay, I'm just trying to be a good mother. Always remember I taught you how to be thrifty and economical. Your sister was grateful for her birthday gift.'

Ali shouted, 'You gave her a toothbrush and a soap!'

'How is Indeerah?'

'Okay, bye.' He did not wait for her to respond and hung up the phone. He checked the receipt, called the bakery and complained that the cake did not have sufficient chocolate. A lady listened to his complaint and eventually decided to offer him a complimentary cake. He gladly accepted and told her, 'America is still a great country.' Within twenty minuted another cake was delivered to his home. He ate the entire cake and drank two bottles of Sprite. Later in the evening he could not move his left arm and the left side of his face was contorted. He became afraid and called his wife. She did not hear. He opened his mouth and shouted. Then he realized that she did not hear his voice.

Indeerah entered his room with a large tray that had five hot dog sandwiches, two milkshakes, six doughnuts and a pack of Oreo cookies. She rested the tray near his feet and could not bear to watch his eating frenzy. He hit the nearby table with his right hand to attract her attention. She looked at the fallen table and then stared at his face. She realized his mouth was twisted and saliva was slowly dripping on his hairy chest. He tried to point to his mouth and paralyzed left arm. Tears rolled down his fat cheeks.

She panicked and a look of fear spread across her face. 'Dear...what's wrong with your mouth? Why are you dribbling?' She knelt beside him and touched his cheek. She then shouted, 'You have a stroke!'

He opened his mouth but could only utter gibberish. She knew something was seriously wrong and quickly dialed 911.

Within seven minutes an ambulance was at their front door. The paramedics were surprised to see the unhealthy and unkempt surroundings. The floor of the living room had fly swatters, old radios, four cracked computer monitors, outdated calendars, crumpled flyers and empty food containers. They could not remove Ali from his room. They called the fire station and requested that a hole be made in the wall of the house. After two hours a crane pulled his bed outside. However, he could not fit in the ambulance and a larger ambulance arrived to transport the obese man. Curious neighbors emerged from their homes. Some had never seen Ali for two years. His skin was pale and the sunlight caused him to squint.

Indeerah returned to his empty room. Chocolate wrappers were scattered on the floor. The bedpan needed emptying. She felt feelings of emptiness, loneliness and freedom. The prison guard had grown attached to the prisoner. The tray with his dinner was on the ground. She carried it to the kitchen and began to sob. Her feelings of hatred had disappeared.

At the hospital, three beds were joined to allow comfortable accommodation for Ali. He had two oxygen tanks near his bedside and tubes connected to his nostrils and arms. This was to assist him in breathing. There were also tubes connected to his chest and an electronic monitor. He missed viewing cable television. Every day, Carla, a

Trinidadian nurse would give him a sponge bath. She would leave work early to watch reruns of the Simpsons. Her brother, Kyle, was a History teacher at a secondary school in Tobago, in the Caribbean. He often visited his sister.

Vladimir and Sumintra visited the hospital. Both felt that Indeerah contributed to their son's poor health condition. Ali opened his eyes and smiled. He had problems breathing and eventually closed his eyes and continued sleeping.

Vladimir began to cry when he saw his son, 'We always try our best to give you the best foods and healthy drinks. How this could happen?' He looked at Indeerah and asked, 'Would the hospital bill be a lot. Does he have health insurance?'

She hesitated. 'No. We did not qualify for Medicaid because my salary is more than $15,000 a year. I could have earned more but some people did not want to hire me because of my tattoos. Last year I told him that life and health insurances are a waste of money. We thought Obamacare would take care of poor people like us. But he did have car insurances with Geico, AllState, 21st century Insurance and the General Automobile Insurance.'

Vladimir stopped crying. 'I didn't realize you earned so little. He had a car? He could drive?'

Indeerah bent her head and said softly, 'No, but he liked the advertisements on cable television and decided to get these insurances just in case in the future we decided to buy a Toyota Corolla car and after we would then take driving lessons.'

Vladimir and Sumintra were shocked and remained speechless. They quickly bid goodbye and exited the hospital.

Three months in the hospital was the wake-up call that Ali and Indeera needed. His cholesterol, blood sugar and blood pressure readings were extremely high. The doctors advised he begin taking daily doses of Niaspan and Zetia. Furthermore, doctors recommended liposuction and lap-band surgery. He agreed to lose weight and was allowed to return home. Indeera obtained samples of the medicine from friends who were pharmacists.

'Honey, I have to go Las Vegas for a few weeks,' said Indeerah.

Ali was surprised. 'But I only returned home two days ago. Why are you going?'

'We cannot afford to pay the hospital bills. So, I've decided to go Las Vegas and see if I could win some money to help pay the bills.'

He smiled. 'That is a very wise decision. I am very lucky to have a wife like you.'

She blushed.

During the next two weeks, he attempted various diets that were recommended. These included the Starvation, Atkins, Cookie, Maple Syrup, Jenny Craig South Beach, Mayo and Cabbage Diets. He tried Super Colon Cleanse and but failed to lose weight. He then began a Tapeworm Diet in which a tapeworm from Africa was allowed to live in him. However, this diet was short-lived because he regularly suffered from diarrhea. He ate sandwiches from Subway but stopped after three days. He was able to lose two pounds and complained the sandwiches made him feel depressed and weak.

He tried Nutrisystem and for breakfast would drink a 6-pack of Ultra Slim Fast, three bottles of Ensure but there were no signs of weight loss. He checked online and joined Weight Watchers and for dinner would eat fifteen Weight Watchers Smart Ones Entrees but after one week stopped the program because of nausea and headaches. He began a diet of wine, pork chops and steak. His tried drinking herbal teas. But he disliked the taste of teas and preferred cups of Swiss Miss Cocoa with marshmallows.

After three weeks in Las Vegas, Indeerah visited her sister in Maryland who lived on the same street with the radio host of Caribbeana. She ate fish and chips at Austin Grill on Ellsworth Drive in Silver Spring. She went to Hyattsville and bought chicken soup from The Original Soupman, six hamburgers from Five Guys Burgers and nine tenderloin steaks from Outback Steakhouse. These foods from Hyattsville were for Ali. Next day she returned home. Ali was watching Hell's Kitchen and did not hear her enter the front door. She placed her suitcases in her room and shouted, 'Honey I'm back.'

Ali was startled. He smiled when he saw his wife enter his room. 'Did you bring any food from Las Vegas and Maryland?' He weighed one thousand pounds.

'Yes, I got two huge hamburgers from the Heart Attack Grill. The meat in one seems to be smelling bad, it could be spoiling because I left it in the car for a few hours. I also got some soup, steaks and hamburgers from Maryland.'

Ali clapped his hands. 'Give them to me. I've been waiting for a long time to eat something from other states in the USA.' He bit into one of the sandwiches. 'Hmm this is delicious. What is the name of these hamburgers from Las Vegas?'

'They are known as quadruple-bypass.'

He hummed whilst eating the two oversized hamburgers. After, he drank a tall cup of Ovaltine and then ate all the foods purchased from Maryland. He still felt hungry. 'Check in the fridge and bring a plate of something, I still feeling hungry and bring the bottle of Coke.' She obliged and returned with a plate of three pancakes, Coke, Jack Daniel's Ribs and Steak from TGI Fridays. After he greedily consumed fried chicken and nine waffles from Roscoe's. Then he said, 'I'm still hungry. Go and make some pancakes.' She made twenty pancakes. After eating one he asked, 'Is this Bisquick pancake mix?'

'Yes dear, you like that.'

Ali shouted, 'No! I always eat Aunt Jemima pancakes. Are you trying to kill me?' He refused to eat them and pushed the plate away.

One month later, Vladimir visited his son and begged him to have gastric bypass surgery to assist in his weight reduction. 'Son, you must try and lose some weight. If you do not get thinner, you will die soon.'

Ali sighed. 'I cannot get thinner because then the government will stop their disability grant and I will be forced to go and find a job. Being fat has its advantages.'

'Really? What advantages?'

'Well when I learn to drive and buy a car, I will be allowed to park in the handicapped zone,' he said, 'but sometimes I wish to be thin.'

His father's nonchalantly asked. 'Really? When? What for?'

'Sometimes I wish I was thin to audition in Dancing with the Stars, The X Factor and America's Got Talent.' He poured Trix into a large bowl of milk.

Vladimir shook his head and did not reply. He left his son and met Indeerah in the kitchen. He pointed to decaying items on the floor and asked, 'Why do you have dried and decaying orange peel?'

'That is for a potpourri I am planning to create. That will freshen the room. It will be healthy because it is home-made.'

He frowned. 'What about the two broken mirrors and four old postboxes in the corner of the living room?'

'Ali will fix those mirrors when he is better. He promised to do so.'

He lifted the clock that was lying on a table and said, 'What about this old clock without hands?' He pointed to items scattered in the corner of the room. 'What plans you got for those three broken bulbs, eleven empty bottles of Downy, eighty empty aerosol Air Wick cans, a twisted lamp, a car door, broken candles and two old fans?'

'Put that down gently. I can sell that clock and the fans at a garage sale. All this stuff got sentimental value so be careful with it.'

'Really? Garage sale? You mean garbage sale. It has people in America who will buy this garbage?'

'Yes, in fact I bought those antique fans on eBay. I plan to get someone to refill the disposable Air Wick cans. I'm hoping that some of these items got historical value and will be featured on Pawn Stars on the History Channel.'

'This radio working?' asked Vladimir.

Indeerah avoided eye contact. 'Of course not. It is an antique.'

He pointed to an old car battery and cynically said, 'I suppose this will also be sold in the garage sale.'

'No, this is more precious and I will see if a pawn shop or thrift shop will pay more for it.'

Vladimir had never seen so much junk. 'What about these broken crutches, two dented car doors, four mannequins, three wigs and three old wheelchairs?'

'Well I plan to get them repaired and keep them in case somebody had an accident in the future and needed crutches or a wheelchair. It could be me or you. Life is so unpredictable. The mannequins tend to frighten away thieves.'

He nodded. He saw flies buzzing around bananas and apples with holes and black skins. He pointed to the decaying fruits on the kitchen counter. 'Why don't you throw those away?'

'No those are for a compost heap. They are biodegradable.'

'Well they look rotten and ready for the heap.' He took the bananas and headed outside.

She shouted, 'I haven't started the compost heap so just leave it anywhere in the backyard. Sometime next year or soon I will start the heap.'

In the backyard he saw broken toys, a television set without a screen, a broken baby crib, damaged birdcages, a guitar with two strings, rusty exercise equipment, a torn trampoline, three soaked and soiled mattresses, empty toothpaste boxes, two cracked computer monitors, a cracked aquarium, four broken flower pots, empty food containers, cracked vases and hundreds of tins that once contained salmon, tuna, beef, spam and beans. Rats and cockroaches scurried among old tires and piles of old magazines and newspapers. He felt nauseous and returned inside the house. He opened the refrigerator and was surprised to see shelves with plates containing decaying food. He pointed to two plates with brown and black foodstuffs. 'What is that?'

'Rice and pasta.'

'Rice? Pasta? Really? Since when is it that color? That should be thrown out.'

Indeerah wanted to end the questioning. 'I spent hard-earned money for all that food. Do you think money does grow on trees? Put back that loaf of bread.'

'The bread has mold and is hard.'

'I will scrape off the mold and when I heat up the bread, it will get soft,' she said in an angry tone.

'Bread is cheap, throw this out and I will buy you all fresh bread.'

'No thanks. That bread you are holding is to make bread pudding.'

'Pudding? For who? Pigs?' Vladimir now realized the reason his son frequently complained of diarrhea and food poisoning.

Ali wanted to be remembered by future generations. He wrote to the Guinness World Records asking that he be considered as the fattest person in the world. They replied that he needed to increase his weight by six pounds to break the record. He was an agnostic but changed. Every night, he earnestly prayed to God for help in achieving this personal goal. His wife was an atheist but decided to temporarily believe in God. Each morning she prayed aloud, 'God please give Ali the strength to reach this milestone. Dear Lord, you know that I don't believe in you, but at least help Ali to gain more weight so he could achieve his dream and fulfill his earthly mission. Amen.'

Chapter 4
Coping with problems

Jose decided to leave his job at the airport because it was stressful. This did not pose a problem because Mabel was making sufficient money to support the family. She supported his decision and also felt that he should not work because he was bipolar. He decided to become an artist and began drawing scenes of skyscrapers and rural landscapes. He worked as a part-time curator at the El Museo del Barrio located on 1230 Fifth Avenue at 104 Street in Manhattan. The museum preserved art and culture of Latin Americans and Puerto Ricans in the United States. He felt honored and donated his diaries, salary receipts and unpublished manuscripts to the museum.

Nikita was twenty five years and had psychological problems. She seldom ventured outdoors and slept in a specially made crib and wore a baby's bib during breakfast, lunch and dinner. She wore Huggies diapers, used Huggies baby wipes, had a teething ring and ate Gerber's baby food that had strained pears, chicken noodle, turkey and rice. During the weekends she ate Heinz strained creole fruits or mixed fruits. On the first day of each month she went to Costco and bought packs of diapers and tins of Nestum, Enfamil and Similac.

Mabel read Standard Classified Nomenclature of Disease and diagnosed Nikita as being psychopathic. She did four counseling sessions with Nikita who seemed to be recovering. However, after three weeks Nikita lapsed into her routine of mimicking a baby. Every morning, she drank milk in a plastic bottle with a feeding nipple. During the day she drank PediaCare and PediaSure. She used Johnson's Baby Shampoo when showering and after rubbed Johnson's Baby Lotion on her arms and legs. Whenever she was ill, she would visit a paediatrician. In 2002, she complained that persons were trying to poison her food. She sometimes vomited after eating and some days refused to eat. She returned to Mabel and was assessed as being paranoid, bulimic and anorexic.

On Valentine's Day in 2003, Nikita began writing letters to a prisoner from Cook County Jail in Chicago. He was a serial killer, of German descent, serving a life sentence. She felt he looked cute in his green prison clothes. After ten months of exchanging letters with the sociopath, Nikita proposed to him. He willingly accepted and they were married during one of her monthly visits. Sumintra was disappointed with her stepdaughter's choice. She wanted Nikita to marry a prisoner of Caribbean origin.

In 2004, the Caribbean was severely affected by Hurricane Ivan. It was one of the rare occasions in the history of the Caribbean in which a high level of unity was displayed. The many divisions - religion, ethnicity, class and gender were put aside as many rallied together to assist the victims. However, amidst the generosity there were disgruntled voices and objections to the assistance offered to the affected islands.

It was a hot day at Pompano Beach in Florida. There were four friends- Gadahar, Stetcher, Shelly and Francine. They missed Trinidad and Tobago.

'Trump?' asked Stetcher. The friends were playing a card game known as All Fours. Three years ago, Francine had taught her friends the rules of the game.

Gadahar stared at the six cards in his hand. 'Stech sorry I have a low piece and the rest is bush.'

Shelly smiled. 'Dat jack going to get hang soon.' Francine nodded. Shelly liked when Francine was her partner in All Fours because Francine usually held high pieces of trump such as the ace, king or queen. The friends used matchsticks to score points for each round of the game.

Gadahar, Stetcher and Shelly occasionally switched to their Caribbean dialect. They had chosen a spot near the shade of the coconut trees. Shelly, the step-sister of Jose, had spent holidays in the Caribbean islands of St. Lucia, Barbados, Cuba and Tobago. Stetcher was a cook in Curry Hut in Margate and worked briefly at The Rise in central Trinidad in 2001. In 2004, Francine met Shelly and Gadahar at a Carnival fete in Miami. Gadahar was a security guard at Bedessee West Indian Supermarket and Tropical Feast Restaurant. He was a former Navy Seal who served in Iraq during the 1990s. Shelly had a degree in Computer Science from Miami Dade College and worked as a secretary at the Latin American and Caribbean Studies Center at Florida International University in Miami. This institution was planning to host an international conference in 2008. She had worked for three years as a waitress at De Islands Restaurant in Coral Springs and Hibiscus Restaurant in Sunrise.

Shelly and Francine won six points for high, low, hang jack game. Francine took six matchsticks and placed it in a pile near to Shelly. She rubbed her eyes. Shelly passed the deck of cards to Gadahar. He shuffled and carefully dealt six cards to each player.

'Trump dis time!' shouted Stetcher.

Francine was collecting signatures for a petition demanding greater Caribbean unity and an end to poverty and unemployment. She obtained signatures at the annual Miss Miami Carnival Pageant at the Bicentennial Park in downtown Miami. She boasted that she recently completed a Masters degree in Clinical Psychology, a certificate in Psychiatry and a diploma in Psychopathology. The three programs were completed in two months and offered by Anonymous International University which was a diploma mill. She also earned extra degree credits because of her experience in counseling. Her counseling experience was partly based on chatting with strangers on the bus and subway. She adjusted the Rayban glasses which slipped to the tip of her nose. She looked at the sky and then turned to the others, 'Aye all yuh see dem horrible pictures on TV larse night of de hurricane victims?'

'Yes it really touched me. Tears run dong my cheeks when I see how much devastation take place in Grenada. All them people's homes destroyed, and the whole island in a mess,' said Gadahar. He opened a bottle of suntan lotion and squirted some into the palm of his hand. He then vigorously rubbed it on his arms and legs. 'It will take that country at least five years to rebuild and recover from that disaster. All their crops and most of the livestock gone. You could imagine living without water and electricity for weeks? Imagine food spoiling, wearing dirty clothes and having to sleep early.'

Stetcher opened the cooler and chose a bottle of Samba beer. 'I cannot bear it. Is jus' too much suffering and inconvenience. Even the prisoners in the jails escape.' He was an illegal immigrant for the past six years. He was medium built and fifty years old. He had a distinct limp and his paunch and flabby arms reflected a comfortable, sedentary lifestyle.

Francine wanted them to appreciate the significance of her group. 'Lissen, before ah forget, ah belong to a group known as Poverty, Unemployment and Racism Eradicated or PURE. The group also promoting Caribbean unity.' She spoke about the group on such radio programs as Sangeet Mala, WHSR (980 am), Fusion Hour, Peter Ganesh Realty Show, Indian Talent on Parade, Hibiscus Moment and Dil-ki-Awaz. 'All yuh might know June from Cuba and Stephanie from de small island of Nevis, two of dem is part of de group. And ah collecting signatures in a petition from all over de USA so ah want all yuh signatures.' She began to eat Doritos Tortilla Chips.

'No problem, give we some sheets, we go sign up,' said Stetcher. He was not interested in her activism. He yawned and asked, 'Anybody want anything to drink?' He felt tired and sleepy. Yesterday he was one of the top spin bowlers in the United States Open T20 cricket competition in Florida. The annual competition was won by United Chargers, a New York-based team. He was a member of Florida Southeast Cricket League. Gadahar was also an avid cricketer and competed in league matches organized by the South Florida Cricket Alliance and the City of North Lauderdale Cricket. He was a left-handed batsman.

Shelly raised her hand and jokingly told him, 'Yes what non-alcoholic things yuh have? Hurry up and come back is your turn to deal now.' She was a teetotaler and regularly chatted with an online friend, via Skype, who owned Joy's Roti Delight in Lauderhill. The friend recently decided to abstain from alcohol when she witnessed its negative effects.

'Coconut water, grapefruit juice and soda water,' said Stetcher. The coconut water was purchased from Ram D'Coconut man 711 Food Store in Margate.

Shelly opened a pack of Honey Maid Grahams. 'I'll take de coconut water. Francine hand meh de sheet to sign.' She played in matches organized by South Florida Softball Cricket. She looked at the cards in her hand and realized she held a bare jack.

Francine checked her cards. She gave Shelly one of the sheets which had four signatures. In a jocular mood she said, 'sister, things bad on dis side but we making a point for low.'

'There are businesses that might be willing to assist,' said Shelly, 'check places like D Pirates Bay, Sati's Indian and Variety Store, Beer Garden, Aqua Lounge and Tropics.'

Francine nodded. 'Thanks. I will be appearing on television on Indi-Caribbean Showcase, Rockers TV and Channels 76 and 79. Yesterday I was interviewed by Laureen Gosine on WVCG 1170 AM.'

'Yes I know her. She served on the board of the T&T USA Chamber of Commerce and also hosted the Mastana Bahar USA competition,' said Shelly. She adjusted her scarf. It was a windy day.

'What else yuh have to drink?' asked Gadahar. He had lost weight and was fifty years old. Seven months ago he was diagnosed with prostate cancer and began chemotherapy. The diagnosis made him appreciate the fragility of life and the need for healthy living. The All Fours game was relaxing and made him temporarily forget his ailment.

Stetcher peered into the cooler and began moving around the drinks. 'Is only Puncheon, and Johnnie Walker? Man, don't waste time, go and bring a bottle of White Oak.'

Gadahar smiled and was slow to respond. 'I is illegal. You forget or what? Check yuh cards quick and tell me if you have trump.' His travel visa had expired.

Francine smiled. 'Look na, jus' because yuh overstay yuh time in de USA doh mean yuh cyah have some alcohol.' Stetcher laughed aloud and did not raise his head to reply and continued searching in the cooler. The ice was not enough and the drinks were not cold.

Shelly interjected, 'Hush and treat him as if he from Alcoholics Anonymous. After this game we will stop, because all yuh man only want to drink and also hardly holding trump.'

'All yuh small islanders not easy na,' said Gadahar, 'anyways, Hurricane Ivan was really a wicked ting. Ah feel sorry for the Prime Minister of Grenada. Ah glad that most of the Caribbean was spared so others could lend a helping hand to their affected beloved neighbours. Ah tell allyuh before and ah go say it again—God must be from de Caribbean.'

'Amen to that,' said Stetcher. He scratched his neck. 'But Shelly why you so quiet? Now look trouble here today.' He slapped his neck and checked the palm of his hand. He had killed a mosquito. He was angry.

Shelly gave him a bottle, 'Here put some of this repellant.'

Stetcher sprayed the repellant on his arms, legs and face. He returned the bottle to Shelly. 'Sometimes I don't think countries like Trinidad should be helping Grenada so much. Look, I does read news on the internet and know Trinidad have plenty crime, water problem, drug trafficking, gangs and unemployment. Yet Trinidad prime minister want to help them damn foreigners.'

Francine placed two ice cubes in her drink. 'Ah agree a little with both of you. All dem stupidee politicians full of gran' charge. Buh how yuh could think so? De longes' rope does have ah end, so jus' now we go have good times. Is because dem Grenadians of African descent? Look at me, I living good with all my friends.'

'I don't want no commess,' said Gadahar. He cleaned his teeth with his index finger. A piece of meat was stuck near his wisdom teeth. 'Why anytime anyone disagrees with a public comment or political action that person is accused of being a racist or a die-hard party supporter? That is why the Caribbean so backward.' He took a toothpick from a glass container and continued cleaning his teeth.

Francine shook her head. 'Is nothing about politics and race. In Trinidad dey have so many damn problems, I was a little girl in Felicity in January 1965 when Dr. Capildeo slam the government's idea of joining with Grenada.'

Shelly was intimidated by her comment. 'Ah eh want to chook fire but look at all de traffic problems on the highways every morning, de massive potholes in de roads, the high rate of murders and kidnappings and….'

Gadahar interrupted her and spoke in an arrogant tone. 'That is true, but it is not a valid reason that the prime minister shouldn't help the other islands affected by the hurricane. All the prime minister wants to do is to help de less fortunate brothers and sisters. Suppose you had family or relatives in Grenada, then what?'

Stetcher was eating frozen yogurt from Red Mango. 'True.' He was not sure of the topic being discussed and who was winning the argument. He was tipsy.

'Come nah Gadahar! Doh play wid me. Suppose you were a Grenadian in Grenada, I'm sure you go want a little assistance,' said Francine. She had both hands on her hips.

'That true too Francine.' Gadahar cleaned his teeth with his right index finger. He opened a cooler and looked at the chicken roti. 'Ah hope allyuh doh chinks on de chicken.' Some of the roti was purchased from D River Cook.

'Nah it have plenty, take one,' replied Francine, 'suppose Trinidad and Tobago was unlucky and we island was devastated.' She coughed and patted her chest. Her throat was dry. 'Ent citizens from there go be happy for some help?' She opened her purse and began searching for a mint.

Shelly watched the waves breaking on the seashore. It was a humid day. 'You are right, I agree I should not be thinking so narrow and only concerned about Trinidad. Is a very selfish way of thinking. It have a Trinidad saying- never mess in de road cause yuh go pass back and mash it.'

'Now yuh talking!' said Francine. She collected the matchsticks and carefully placed them in a small box.

Shelly looked at the food on Stetcher's plate. 'Aye, eat up the roti, you know is better your belly buss than good food waste.' She placed more food on his plate. 'Here eat de potato pie, it come from Gopaul's Vegetarian and de coconut drops from Kidd's Island Bakery and Restaurant Shed. So how tings with yuh Trini girlfriend? De girl you pick up last year in North Stand for Carnival.'

'I spend a few months down there and was tackling Nadine who I meet in First & Last Bar in Chaguanas during my trip. About six months now we break up. And ah did buy ah new car to show off with she.' He slowly placed both hands behind his head and rocked back on the beach-chair. 'I was real bazodee over she. I was she doux doux darling.'

'How yuh leh dat pass through your hand?'

He began to wring his hands. 'De whole village down in Chaguanas did know 'bout meh tabanca. She give meh a six for a nine. Dat bitch was horning me with the obzokee dougla from Tunapuna.'

Shelly had a surprised look. 'Wait na, but ent dat dougla married? Yuh know cutlass doh leave mark in water.'

'Yeah buh he wife doh care. When de mark buss I end up losing. I gone by he house and tell dougla wife and she start to planasse me in front of everybody.'

'WHAT? Yuh makin' joke. She is ah old duttyness.' She wanted to laugh at his predicament but instead felt pity.

His face reflected a heart-broken man. 'No, is true. De story was in the weekly tabloids- Sunday Punch and Friday Mirror. And like he doesn't have any shame, imagine he gone by my friend who I was staying by a few days after to buy parc water and bois bandé.'

Shelly patted his back. 'Dat real depressin' boy, forgeh dem. We up here in the U.S. Come leh we go and buy some roti.' Stetcher returned a petition sheet to Francine. Shelly reminded the others to invite interested persons to the conference next year. Both Shelly and Stetcher bid goodbye to their friends and departed. They went to LC's Roti Shop at Caribbean Shoppes Plaza in North Miami-Dade. It was a long drive but they were not bothered.

Shelly ordered buss-up-shut and side dishes of curried channa, potato and chicken. She watched in awe as the dough was layered and folded a few times. Ghee was brushed on with each fold and this gave the buss-up-shut a nice flaky texture. She wanted to learn the art of making this type of roti.

Stetcher requested dhalpuri with shrimp. The waitress gave them their food and condiments. He carefully placed a few drops of hot sauce on the side of his plate and said, 'This shop use to be on Biscayne Boulevard…somewhere near 81st Street.'

Shelly took kucheela and added it to her food. 'No I did not know that. This is the first time I'm coming here.' She had a glass of sorrel. 'I feel it really have too much hate in Trinidad and Tobago and even Guyana. Some ignorant people does be pushing a race head and that does keep the people ignorant.' She licked her fingers. 'Man this curry nice too bad. Is up to people like Francine to help educate de people. The Caribbean diaspora cannot solve the problems of the West Indies. By the way who yuh vote for in de larse election?'

He was hesitant in replying. 'Republican of course. I is ah Republican till ah dead. What about you?'

'Democrats.' She was pensive. 'For awhile I was supporting the Tea Party.' She wondered if Caribbean people in United States supported the Democrats. 'Is time dis country get a black president.'

He sipped on a young coconut. It reminded him of coconut water he frequently drank at Lucky City Restaurant. Before leaving he thought about dinner and decided to order some bara, a sada roti with conch and a dhalpuri with vegetables. After they went to the Publix Supermarket at Lantana Plaza and bought cantaloupe, cheddar cheese, Pinot Noir, Chardonnay and Cabernet. After Stetcher left, Shelly went to Costco and was surprised to see caskets were on sale. She ordered the Lady of Guadaloupe and Kentucky Rose Caskets. She provided the cashier with her completed form and paid using her credit card. That evening she placed both caskets in her garage. She went inside and checked online to see the costs of tombstones.

At Pompano Beach, Gadahar turned to Francine and said, 'Ah wish odder people would be so willing to change their views and look at dis natural disaster as a sign from God for us to unite and be thankful for our survival.' He stopped and laughed. 'Stop watching meh with yuh coki-eye as if I is a prophet.'

'Me? Man is real sense yuh talk. From today I going to encourage others to change their views. From today I cool like Gokool.' Francine lit a cigarette. She asked, 'Yuh finish sign de petition? Wha' yuh waitin' on – Christmas?'

Gadahar handed her the paper. 'Yeah, here look de sheet. You should also check the Hindu Temple of South Florida and the Amar Jyoti Mandir in Miami, also the Shiva Mandir in Oakland Park. These have some Caribbean people who will be glad to sign. I'm a member of the New Sensations Tassa Group and will ask them to support this effort.'

'Okay, thanks.'

He glanced at his watch. 'Well ah better be going now. If ah not home by ten o'clock Dorothy does geh on like a sketelle. When yuh miss me, ah gone.' His girlfriend was the sister of Indeera.

Francine laughed. 'Hurry up man, or else crapaud smoke yuh pipe.' She looked at him and said aloud, 'Gadahar you really eat de bread dat the Devil knead. Is so you stop. Ah know your girlfriend doh bite nice. Ah hear you does have to geh yuh passport stamp before yuh leave de house.' She playfully pushed him. 'Don't worry you in Florida and not Trinidad.'

Gadahar had a sad expression. He remembered his adulterous wife. 'Next year we have to organize a longer beach lime.'

Francine waved. 'Ah go see yuh laters, ah have to go home and pack meh suitcase, meh flight to Grenada is 6.30 tomorrow morning.'

'Buh wha' is de rush? Is Caribbean Airlines yuh flying with. You ever remember dem leaving on time?' He smiled. 'Gyul dat flight bong to be delayed till late in de night or next day.'

She laughed. 'Is true buh yuh know ah eh want to take no chances, since is not my money dat buy de ticket.' She left and quickly headed for her car. She felt her visit to Florida was a success.

'Have a safe trip!' Gadahar shouted, 'good luck with getting dem signatures. Bring back a good woman for meh!' He remained and watched the sunset. He thought about death.

Chapter 5
Return to the Caribbean

Francine arrived at Grenada's airport which now seemed small. She had grown accustomed to the airports in the United States. After collecting her luggage and exiting Customs, she was greeted by Bertha, a resident of Grenada. Bertha was elderly and wiped tears trickling down her cheeks. 'Oh gawd, why this happen to meh beloved country! So much innocent people suffer and dead. The National Stadium and Parliament destroyed.'

Francine sought to offer consolation and hugged her. 'I have some financial donations which would assist persons.' Beads of sweat were on her forehead. She wiped her brow and wished she had used more deodorant. She fanned herself with a small handkerchief.

Bertha did not seem to care. She blew her nose in a small towel. 'Look at de coconut trees scattered like toothpicks and all de houses and dem without roofs.'

Francine offered her a handkerchief and patted her back. 'Gyul doh worry, ah know all yuh Grenadians have a fighting spirit and will get tings going again. Doh ever forgeh dat God is a good God, he go never give yuh a burden dat yuh cyah carry.'

Nearby was Jestina who was sporting short dreadlocks. 'Meh parents work so hard to build a home and it totally mash up. How ah go survive? De bank eh go len' me no money since I lorse meh job larse year.'

Francine offered her comforting words, 'God go find ah way for all de suffering people.'

Maurice also heard the conversation. 'Excuse me marm, I could not help overhearing your sad plight. I am a politician from St. Vincent and I have a meeting this evening with the Prime Minister of Grenada. We are going to discuss the situation and seek international assistance….' He was fat, balding and forty years old.k

Jestina began to beat her chest. 'Ah is jus' ah poor graduate student who scrunting to make ends meet. Ah doh have any money in de bank to fix meh home. It was ah special home- it had no doors inside the home. Yes, no doors in each room because ah didn't want my two girl chirren sleeping with no man. Dey is only teenagers. If I cyah sleep with a man den dey should not be sleeping with man. How ah little island, which smaller than Grenada could assist? Ent St. Vincent and the Grenadines was also damaged by de hurricane?'

'Yes, those islands were affected. Marm what's your name?' asked Maurice. He was concerned that Jestina and Bertha were so emotional.

'Meh name is Jestina Gobin.'

Maurice said, 'Well Jestina, there is an old saying in my country that one-one does full basket. This means that if the Caribbean neighbors could all contribute a small amount to each of the affected islands, things will improve.'

Bertha nodded, 'Pardon my interruption mister but I agree with you...we can all help.'

'That's right,' said Francine. She looked at Jestina, Maurice and Bertha and said in a weary voice, 'Lissen everybody, ah almost forgeh, ah collecting signatures for a petition which will be presented to prime ministers at the Caricom meeting next year. And, ah was wondering if ah could get all yuh signatures. De petition is to end poverty, unemployment and racism.'

Maurice smiled. He placed a chewing gum in his mouth. 'Sure, give me a few sheets to get support from other people.'

Francine handed him the sheets. 'Here look fifty sheets, and dis is meh group's postal address in Trinidad for yuh to post de sheets when yuh it fill up.'

He neatly folded the stack of sheets. 'Okay will pass it around to friends and family.'

Bertha extended her arm, 'Yes, I'll sign and ah could take a few for meh son and daughter schools.'

'And where you from Jestina?' asked Maurice.

'I was born in Barbados but for the past seventeen years I living in the United States,' said Jestina, 'my parents living in Grenada for the last forty years. I have a small home here and would stay in it when I return for the holidays.' She migrated to Los Angeles in 1988 and had an undergraduate degree in International Relations from the University of California and was enrolled to pursue a Masters degree in Mass Communications at State University of New York in Buffalo. However, last year she had a change of heart and dropped out of the program. Five years ago she registered for a Masters degree at the Center for Latino, Latin American and Caribbean Studies at Albany University in New York. Her thesis topic was 'The Effect of Inter-racial Marriages between Latin Americans and West Indians, 1980-2004.'

'So what yuh doing back here? Visiting family?' asked Bertha.

'No, I came to do some research for a conference on media and culture which will be held next month at Florida International University,' said Jestina.

'Yes, I heard about it from a friend in Florida,' said Francine.

Jestina wanted to sign the sheet. 'May I borrow your pen? So how tings Francine?'

Francine lent her a pen. 'Dire dire, nothing new dese days. De odder day ah read dat nearby Barbados planning to stop havin' de Queen as their head of state.'

'So dey say, but dat is something dat could just be ole talk from those politicians.'

Bertha said in a jocular tone, 'Our medical school in Grenada is truly a wonderful institution. Students from all across the Caribbean and even abroad are becoming doctors. Now doctors knockin' dog. All the social, family and educational ties abroad will greatly assist in rebuilding Grenada. Don't forget the so-called solid political ties de politicians always boasting about with international leaders. Maybe these leaders will help.'

'I eh know about solid political ties!' said Francine, 'de only ties dem politicians know about is ties for dey expensive suits, Yesterday I read the newspapers claiming, that my Trinidadian prime minister planning to send some workers to Grenada.'

Jestina and Bertha laughed.

Maurice said, 'Yes, is sanitation workers who will assist in clearing away trees that blocking roads and had fallen on homes. I'm not exactly sure of their role.'

There was a public announcement on the microphone for passengers to board the plane.

'So how much signatures yuh have so far?' asked Jestina.

Francine paused and closed her eyes. 'About 200,000 and every day it sort of slowly increasing. Ah got about five hundred signatures in Grenada larse month. After this ah going Cayman Islands, Montserrat, Dominica and Aruba.'

'If is one thing we Caribbean people have is ah sense of humor,' said Bertha, 'all yuh make meh feel so much better, ah really believe now that this Caribbean unity thing will work.'

Francine grabbed her purse. 'Bye everyone, let's keep in touch.'

'Yes, ah will e-mail yuh, bye,' said Maurice

'Bye, good luck with the petition,' said Jestina.

Bertha shouted, 'Bye!'

At the airport, Francine enjoyed duty-free shopping. Amidst the crowd in the airport, she was a forlorn figure. She bought Lindt, Droste, Toblerone and Boticelli chocolates. She heard a flight announcement and began to frantically search her purse. 'Damn! Where de hell is meh boarding pass? Where de hell is meh e-ticket?' She eventually found her ticket, grabbed her suitcase and rushed to the counter.

'Miss you have to check in your luggage before you get a boarding pass'

Francine was confused. 'Before? Since when? This is a new law?'

'No, it is always so. All over the world it is so.'

The clerk checked the weight of her red suitcase and tagged it. She checked her computer.

'Wait! Before you send it off, ah want to hug it.'

The clerk said in a stern voice, 'Pardon me marm. What did you say?'

Francine bent and tightly hugged her red suitcase and then lovingly kissed it. 'Ah will see you soon.' She looked at the clerk. 'I have a very special connection with my purse, umbrella and suitcase.'

The clerks and other passengers were surprised. An employee of the airline threw the red suitcase on a conveyor belt to be packed on the airplane. Francine was shocked to witness the rough handling of her suitcase. She threatened to sue the employee.

Francine cautiously boarded the steps of the plane and complained of arthritis. She patiently listened to the instructions of the airhostess. After takeoff, she called the airhostess, 'Yuh serving any food? What about peleau? Crab and callaloo?'

'No marm. It's a short flight and this is American Airlines.'

Francine shook her head. 'What? Dat is unbelievable! What about water or a soft drink?' She was sweating profusely.

'No. we had to have some cutbacks. But we will serve you if you are dying.'

Francine said, 'Lissen yuh see this liferaft stupidness and fancy mask for my face if oxygen get low…well all dat not important. Ah could do without dat buh certainly not some food and drink. All airlines should know dat Caribbean people like to eat, drink and overload the plane with their luggage.' She wiped her forehead.

The airhostess checked her watch. 'Miss I have good news for you?'

'What?' She rolled her eyes. 'You found some food? You have shark and bake?'

The airhostess frowned. 'No, we will be arriving in two minutes. Read the free in-flight magazine.'

Francine steupsed and stomped her feet. 'This is de larse time ah travelling with allyuh cheap airlines. The plane arrived in the Cayman Islands. She slowly disembarked and was surprised to see the damage after Hurricane Ivan. After she exited the airport she met a policewoman, Roma, and said, 'Ah can't believe meh eyes to see dese big samaan trees ripped from the ground. Hmpf, dese Cayman Islands people must be was real lucky to be alive, look at all dem telephone and electricity poles looking like matchsticks on the road.'

Roma replied, 'Dis damage in the Cayman Islands is something eh gyul?'

She wiped sweat from her brow. 'De Caribbean Disaster Emergency Relief Agency helping plenty. Ah cannot believe meh eyes, it looks like a real nightmare.'

'Yuh accent sounds familiar, yuh from Dominica or Grenada?' asked Francine.

Roma laughed. 'Neither, buh yuh close, I from St. Lucia. We in St. Lucia was slightly affected, about a dozen homes lost roofs, a few homes in the coastal areas lost their walls and were flooded. But we okay. We real blessed.'

Francine nodded. 'Gyul, that island is something yes - allyuh produce two Nobel Prize winners. What is allyuh secret?'

Roma was quiet and then said, 'Ah eh no myself. As soon as ah find out yuh go know, ah could do with some of dat big money dat comes with the prize.'

A blind man with one arm, wearing shades and with a walking stick approached the two women.

'Good evening uncle,' said Francine.

'Hello. Good day marm,' said the blind man.

Roma asked, 'You need any help?'

'No I'm okay, for years I blind but can easily find my way around with the help of my trusty cane.' He scratched under his arm. 'I find everyone is so busy and not often they are helpful like you.'

'Well people busy cleaning up after de hurricane,' said Roma, 'is furse time ah ever hear about this type of massive destruction.'

'Eh, eh ah glad ah meet all yuh people here. Leh meh bother all yuh for a few minutes,' said Francine. She took a small colorful handkerchief from her bosom and wiped her forehead. 'Lawd, this place hot for so. Meh name is Francine and ah belongs to a group from Trinidad and Tobago dat collecting signatures to indicate that de grassroots people, de working class, middle and upper classes all want Caribbean unity and we also want to end poverty, racism and unemployment. Dey want to do dis because…because it go benefit we.'

They were interrupted by Aaron who had his Green Card. He was a drug dealer who distributed marijuana and crystal meth. He was wanted by the Drug Enforcement Agency and was followed by a CIA Clandestine Officer. Before migrating to the United States, he was a street-gang member and drug pusher in San Juan, in north Trinidad. He had underworld connections in Gonzales, Duncan Street, Caledonia, Nelson Street and Diego Martin. He eventually became a notorious gang leader who received government contracts through the Unemployment Relief Programme. He was elusive and never went to jail. However, due to the gang wars to control his turf, he was forced to migrate.

His mother, Delisa, was a crack addict who was bipolar and an illegal alien. For the past six years she resided in Denver, Colorado. Last week, Aaron cynically told her that crack was a Black man's drug and that it was better to smoke marijuana. He laughed at Francine's petition. 'Tings like signatures and letters to the editor of newspapers doh make a difference in the Caribbean. By the way how much signatures yuh have so far?'

'About one million so far. Ah hoping dat de petition could make a positive change in de Caribbean and beyond.'

'WHAT! Dat is plenty, plenty, plenty names,' said Aaron, 'dat is really plenty gyul. I never knew dere was so much people in de region and dat we people wanted unity. Since ah small ah always hearing about how the reasons dat Federation break up in the late 1950s was because of jealousy between Trinidad and Jamaica. And, dat dese countries were very afraid dat small islanders would ah come in thousands and live in their countries.' He lit a joint of marijuana and exhaled a cloud of smoke. He looked at the cloud disappear and felt calm. Smoking was one of his traits of being a man in the Caribbean. He thought about the set-up men in Trinidad who pulled the trigger whenever he called the shot on someone. In his homeland he was protected and had the police on his payroll. He missed his friends in Trinidad and recently met some who migrated to the United States. His friend, Stetcher, who had recovered from cancer and now afflicted with Lou Gehrig's. He was confined to a wheelchair.

Roma said, 'Hand me dat paper leh meh sign meh name.' She paused and looked at Aaron. 'So what you here for?'

Aaron said, 'I have a big foundation in the United States. I'm here to open two orphanages and give three scholarships to needy students in the university and secondary school. I also plan to donate money to persons who want to rebuild their homes.' It was an attempt to get respect. Money talked. 'I will help get names for your petition. Okay you all, nice meeting everyone.'

'Dat accent sounding as if yuh from Trinidad,' said Roma, ' like you is a fresh water Yankee?'

Aaron laughed. 'Darling I aint no yankee.' The blind man left them and headed to a parlour. He purchased a vanilla cupcake and soft drink. Aaron looked at him and twisted his mouth. 'Looks are very deceiving. Dat man doh seem blind like a bat. All ah dem young boys want to be a sweet man or saga boy and de men fighting to be de village ram. If dat blind man had even one eye or half an eye he go be sooting both of you and giving allyuh sweet talk to get allyuh in bed.'

Francine smiled. 'Is true. Well sorry to rudely rush away buh ah have plenty collecting to do in de next three days. Remember whenever all yuh visit Tcrinidad make sure and check meh out.' She gave them small bits of paper. 'Here look meh cell phone number and address.'

'Bye, ah go check yuh next year for Carnival,' said Roma, 'doh worry de people here real friendly, yuh go enjoy meeting dem and collecting names.'

'Yeah later,' said Aaron. He opened a cheque book and began writing. It was a cheque for two thousand dollars. He gave it to Francine, then closed his pen and placed the book in his pants pocket. 'Ah coming for Christmas so make sure yuh cook a little extra ham, pastelles and black cake and have some extra sorrel and gingerbeer.'

She laughed and eagerly accepted the cheque. 'Listen before ah leave ah want to invite all of you to a big conference at Florida International University in August next year. If yuh free come to it…it dealing with the media and culture in the Caribbean. Anyway bye you all.' She left and headed for an apartment building.

Aaron turned to Roma. 'Yes, as ah was saying. I doubt that all men are good. Think about it, ent you have a fadda, brudda or male cousins?'

'I actually have six faddas, four are former step faddas and two kick de bucket. I have nephews and seven brothers, and four male cousins,' said Roma.

'All ah dem bad?' asked Aaron. He lit another joint and puffed.

She was pensive for a few moments and then said, 'Now that you mention it, they really not that bad. Some are dem is some good for nutting but some are kinda helpful. And one is ah real ma commère man.' She suddenly became excited. 'Yuh see, praise God! Amen! Hallelujah! Yuh finally seeing de light!'

Aaron was quick to respond and did not seem to sympathize the men's movement, 'But the majority of men are bad, look at de Caribbean politicians - they are so corrupt. Papa Doc and Baby Doc in Haiti tief money and put it in foreign bank accounts. And since the 1950s, is politicians in Guyana and Trinidad who promoting racism.'

'I wasn't arrong to judge dem but ah does hear some real nasty tings 'bout dem,' said Roma, 'is very sad, but we have to move on. We can't allow the ugly sins of the past to destroy the present and ruin the future. Long time, meh fadder used to tell me and me brudders- every day fuh tief one day fuh police.' She sighed.

'Yuh tink we need to develop a new generation of leaders?' asked Aaron.

Roma replied, 'Exactly! Dat is the only way that gender and race relations will improve. Only then the Caribbean society will progress. Look how de rain set up na.'

She looked at her watch. 'Oh, gosh ah late ah have to pick up meh chirren who gone for lessons. Leh meh ketch a taxi.' She waved her hand to stop a taxi. 'If yuh free anytime come and visit. I living by the third mango tree it have yellow croton in de yard.'

Aaron waved his hand and laughed. 'Okay.'

Roma entered the taxi and exclaimed, 'Buh wait na! What trouble is this! Well wonders never cease. I could ah swear dis taxi driver is de one-arm, blind man who I just pass down the road. Buh ah could be wrong.'

The blind taxi driver said, 'Yes is me.' She opened the door and exited the taxi. He shouted, 'Yuh arse too happy.'

Chapter 6
Life in New York

Francine made short visits to Montserrat, St. Maarten, Dominica and Aruba. She returned to New York, in the USA, to obtain financial support from West Indians. She appeared on West Indian television programs including LMN Television on Channel 507 and Caribbean Spotlight which aired on Sunday evenings on Channel 77. She was also a guest on Let's Talk with Lakshmee on Channel 96 and The Bhanwanie Singh Show on Monday on Channel 77. She was interviewed on four radio stations- the Indo American Show on WPAT, Jodha Talk Show and Dave West Indian Radio Show on 1240 AM WGBB, and the Indo Caribbean Radio Station WICR 1620 AM.

Sunita and her husband, Deo, lived in New York during 1978 to 2009. They returned to their homeland, Trinidad and Tobago in January 2010 but experienced religious and racial discrimination. They decided to return to New York in April 2011. Sunita enjoyed listening to Sounds of Music on 1240 AM WGBB and Best by Request Show on Sunday mornings on WPAT 930 AM. She was a devout Hindu and one of the founding members of the Vedic Dharma of New York which was established in 1981. Four years later, this organization changed its name to Arya Samaj USA. Upon her return she joined a Vedic mandir located at Richmond Hill in Queens. Her daughter, Lalita, was vocalist who sang classical Indian songs and her son, Avinash, was skilled in playing the tabla and dholak. Lalita hoped to participate in the Miss T&T NY competition which would be held at Pace University. The family enjoyed the Hawan and Sandhya mantras.

Deo also attended the nearby Raj Yoga Center and participated in the annual Street Prachar on 121st Street and Liberty Avenue which involved bhajan singing and chanting of mantras. Participants were treated to free refreshments.

Sunita saw Francine on the television and also heard of her work on the radio. Five days later, she contacted Francine and invited her to speak at the mandir. Francine agreed and met Sunita and they went to the mandir. After they went to the Kaiteur Restaurant and Bar and purchased a shrimp roti.

Francine read the poster on the wall. It was an advertisement for a Talent Competition at Smokey Oval Park on 127 Street and Atlantic Avenue in Richmond Hill. 'This is something I should attend. I would be able to meet many West Indians and get a lot of signatures.'

Sunita read it and agreed. 'It's not far from here, I will arrange transport. Last year I attended a Phagwa parade at Smokey Park. It was colorful and I sensed so much joy and unity.' She pointed to another poster. 'This might also be of interest.' It was a public invitation to commemorate East Indian Arrival in the Caribbean.

Francine also read the flyer. 'Have you heard the musical band that will be playing?'

'Yes, the Sansar Sangeet Orchestra is well known and I believe they are located in Richmond Hill. I've heard them play in parties and weddings,' said Sunita, 'Ah hear that somewhere near have a Trinidad and Tobago Street.'

'Wow! The Caribbean have a big presence up here.'

After the meal, both women exited the restaurant and headed for the subway. Sunita said, 'I've found an apartment for you to stay in during the next two weeks.'

'Thanks very much. I am grateful for your hospitality.'

Sunita continued, 'It's located at 101 Avenue in Ozone Park. My cousin Geeta Ramsundar lives there but she is visiting a sick cousin who is in the public hospital in Missouri. She works at Star Party Rental on Sheridan Boulevard and when she returns I will carry you there. Geeta is also a single mother and her son recently graduated from Richmond Hill High School, he is now at Colgate University.'

Francine nodded. The subway train stopped and they exited the train and station. Sunita pointed to three skyscrapers. 'It's the middle one.' They entered the compound and went up the elevator. Sunita opened the door of the apartment and Francine entered.

'I like it. It's roomy and quiet,' said Francine.

Sunita pointed to the refrigerator and showed her the bathroom and living room. She gave her the keys and then departed.

Next day, Francine attended a cricket match at Baisley Park in Queens. It was a game between the Indo-Caribbean Federation Select XI vs Nizam Hafiz Memorial XI. The players were mostly Indo-Guyanese and Indo-Trinidadians. She was able to obtain five hundred and twelve signatures. She regularly bought food from a West Indian Roti Shop at Rockaway Boulevard. She enjoyed the saltfish, parata roti, baigan choka, oxtail and dhalpuri. However she was disappointed the shop did not serve geera pork and black pudding.

Dorothy never learnt to cook the food that Terrance enjoyed. Both were migrants who resided in Queens in New York. He was from Trinidad and Tobago and worked as an insurance agent in Manhattan and she was a housewife. She was divorced and had been married to Gadahar. She could not cook rice and after it was burnt would tell him it was fried rice. After burning the chicken she would tell him it was fried chicken. Two neighbours tried to teach her how to cook but she never remembered the procedures. She could make one dish- macaroni and cheese. And this soon became a dish which Terrance and Dorothy ate four times each week. She consumed a significant amount of canned and frozen foods for breakfast, lunch and dinner.

Dorothy regularly visited her Trinidadian neighbor, Carla, who taught her how to prepare healthy dishes. She entered Carla's home and began admiring the trinkets and ornaments on the shelf. Carla was in the kitchen and said, 'Yes, those came from different parts of the world.' Dorothy quickly snatched two trinkets and placed them in her purse.

Dorothy did not want to assist but wanted to look at the preparation. She complained, 'Anytime ah peel garlic my fingers burn and de potatoes are too difficult to peel. One time while peeling ah potato ah nearly cut off a finger. Ah doh like to clean dasheen bush because it does stain meh fingernails.' She grabbed a spoon and container of salt and quickly placed them in her pockets.

Carla checked the clock. She had fifty minutes to shower, change her clothes and reach to the hospital. Her patient was Ali. He complained of chest pains and was rushed to the hospital. She pulled into the car park and headed for the entrance.

As a result of her terrible cooking skills, Terrance was forced to enroll in cooking courses. Most of his monthly income was spent on purchasing food from Chinese restaurants, the nearby deli and West Indian roti shops. On mornings he would stop at Singh's Roti Shop on 118th Street on Liberty Avenue and buy doubles and roti with bodi, bhagi or pumpkin. He also purchased his lunch- aloo pies, chow mein or peleau. Most evenings he bought baked chicken and macaroni pie for dinner.

Also, his secretary began cooking lunch and dinner for him. His acceptance of these meals soon developed into an extramarital affair. Dorothy knew of the infidelity but neither demanded a divorce nor accused him of any wrongdoing. She was a meek housewife and did not want to seek employment outside the home. She thought about the repercussions of a divorce and did not want to jeopardize her comfortable lifestyle of having a home, car and yearly holidays.

'I have so much responsibilities at home,' she muttered.

Her husband quickly replied, 'Yuh always saying that. You is a real ungrateful wretch. I doing all the work and buying everything in this house!' Due to the regular eating of oily and greasy foods, he suffered from high levels of cholesterol and his wife became diabetic. Additionally, their two children, Nasha and Allan were overweight.

Dorothy did not reply to her husband. She asked her daughter, 'Is that another engagement ring?'

Nasha blushed. 'Yes, my new fiancé gave me last week.' Nasha wore expensive rings and would boast of imaginary boyfriends and fiancés.

'What happened to Alejandro? Did you break up with him?' asked Dorothy. She looked at Natasha's ungainly figure and thought that she was fortunate that men were interested in marrying her.

There was a sad look on Nasha's face. 'Alejandro was a doctor and died in a car accident. He was tall, muscular, blue eyes and blond hair.'

Dorothy feigned sympathy. 'I'm sorry to hear about the tragedy.' She had grown accustomed to hearing tall tales of Nasha's boyfriends and fiancés being killed in accidents, murdered or met their demise by suicide. 'I hope he lives long enough for us to meet him and for you to marry him.' Nasha nodded and quickly left her home. She headed for the mall to buy a new ring.

Three months later, on Valentine's Day, a floral arrangement was delivered to Nasha's home. The card stated- 'From Rawle with lots of love.' Dorothy thought it was a wrong delivery and asked the courier to check the address. He checked and confirmed it was correct. Nasha slowly descended the stairs and saw the expensive bunch of flowers on the dining table. She smiled and clapped her hands. She excitedly said, 'Who sent it?'

'It's from Rawle. Maybe it's a wrong delivery. We'll keep it until someone calls to explain the mix-up. I hope it's not from another stalker.' Dorothy frowned and placed the flowers in two vases.

'Rawle! Yes, I know him.' She closed her eyes and lowered her voice. 'He's my latest boyfriend.'

Terrance was watching television. He partially heard the conversation between his daughter and wife. He suspected that his daughter was living in a fantasy world of romance. He was aware that she regularly ordered flowers for herself and boasted to everyone it was from her boyfriend.

Dorothy was relieved. 'Good I'm glad that is cleared up. Why don't you invite him over for dinner or for a barbecue. He seems like a nice boy and we would like to meet him.'

'He recently moved from Wisconsin and is a bit shy. He is slim and drives a Mercedes Benz. His father owns a chain of pizza stores. Maybe later but I'm meeting him for lunch at the mall. I'll tell him about the invitation. He sent me a really nice email yesterday and I'll forward it to you.' Nasha also created fake email accounts, Instagram, Twitter and Facebook pages in the names of these imaginary boyfriends and would connect them to her friends or print the messages for her mother to read.

For a decade such scenarios would be a normal routine. She would fabricate elaborate stories of wealthy, charming boyfriends and educated fiancés. To make the stories plausible she would regularly buy rings and jewelry and send flowers to her home.

Terrance was in the study room checking his income tax forms. He opened the laptop computer and switched it on. He began browsing the online edition of the three daily newspapers of Trinidad and Tobago. He was surprised to read that the government was planning to release fifty prisoners as part of the country's observance of fifty years of Independence status. He felt this was foolish because of the island's high murder rate.

Dorothy passed near the study. She had a basket overflowing with dirty clothes. She checked pockets before placing them in the washer machine. Her hand touched something in a pocket of Terrance's jeans. She thought it was money but was shocked to discover it was a contraceptive. They had never used this method of birth control. She felt light-headed. She knew of the consequences but decided to confront him.

After regaining her composure, she shouted, 'Ah found something in yuh pocket which we never use.'

Terrance was reading the sports page. He was not aware of her discovery and thus did not realize the seriousness of her statement. 'What honey? A cookbook?'

Dorothy remained quiet and then began crying. She ran into the bedroom and locked the door.

Nasha heard the argument. She whispered to herself, 'Thank God my fiancé is not like that. And when we are married I know he will always be faithful.' She checked her three cellphones for text messages.

Dorothy and Terrance refused to seek marriage counselling. Instead, they willingly appeared on the Steve Wilkos Show and aired their problems. She was publicly humiliated and had to see a therapist. She decided to improve her lifestyle and pursued short courses in Computer Graphics, Spanish, French, Italian Cooking, Typing, Hindi, Etiquette and Business Management. At the end of each program, she received a certificate. She ensured each certificate was framed and placed on the wall in the living room. She wanted Terrance to be aware of her achievements but he continued to ignore her.

The time spent pursuing the courses proved to be her excuse for not cooking and neglecting household chores. Once a month the floor was swept and mopped. Piles of unwashed dishes sometimes remained in the sink for four or five days. Dorothy told her friends and neighbours, 'I only eat fresh food.' At restaurants she would ask the waiter or waitress to see the chef. She would ask the chef or cook, 'I want to see how the food is prepared.' After seeing the preparation then she would be satisfied and return to her table. At Texas de Brazil, a waiter bought a complimentary glass of water. She asked him, 'What type of water is this?'

'Filtered water,' he replied.

'I only drink purified bottled water. Don't insult me. I only eat and drink the best. Take it away immediately.'

After fifteen years of marriage, Dorothy decided to seek counseling from Mabel. Mabel opened an office in Manhattan. On the shelves of her office were past issues of the Canadian Journal of Psychiatry and publications from the American Psychiatric Association. As a result of obtaining more qualifications, the cost of counseling services had increased to four hundred dollars per hour. Dorothy paid for ten hours of counseling. During the first session Mabel advised Dorothy on health issues. 'First, I want you to stop taking all vitamins.' She began writing in her notepad.

'Why? I spent a lot of money buying big bottles of multivitamins and lots of supplements,' replied Dorothy. She took a pencil and pen from the table and quickly placed them in her bag.

'Well, my many years of research and accurate diagnoses have proved that all these vitamins make people mad or crazy. It also leads to a hypersexual disorder.' Mabel was a pathological liar and delusional. She believed that watching reruns of comedies as Frasier, Web Therapy and Anger Management would be educational and make her a professional therapist.

Dorothy smiled. Her body language had changed. She was more defensive. She thought Mabel was being facetious. 'For true?'

Mabel was serious. 'Yes, it's not a joke. Stay away from vitamins and you will feel the difference. Let us meet again next month.' She checked her diary and confirmed the date. She also made an appointment to receive the Zostavax vaccine for the painful shingles.

After the session, Dorothy left the room and paused in the waiting room. She waited for the receptionist to answer the phone and then she quickly took five magazines and shoved them in her bag. She was a kleptomaniac.

On weekends Dorothy purchased West Indian foods which Terrance enjoyed. She regularly shopped at such supermarkets as Western Beef, Met, Pathmark, Key Foods and Bravo. At Key Foods, she asked one of the attendants, 'Allyuh have a shelf with canned and frozen foods from Trinidad and the Caribbean?'

The attendant smiled. 'Yes, that is the home-sick section, it is two aisles to the left. It have foods and drinks.'

She walked to the aisle and saw bottles of Solo, a popular soft drink of Trinidadians. There was a light film of dust on the bottles. The price was US$3 and she felt this was reasonable because it was an imported item and shipping charges were added to the final price. She placed five in her grocery cart and secretly hid one in her purse. She examined a bottle of Matouk's Mauby. There was no expiry date. She placed three bottles in her cart. She headed for the cashier and paid for the drinks. After exiting, he went to the pharmacy and purchased three medicines- Biktarky, Jardiance and Entresto. The Jardiance pills were for her husband who was diabetic and Entresto was for her heart palpitations. The Biktarky was for a neighbour who was recently diagnosed with HIV. When she returned home, the items from the grocery bag and her purse were placed in a cupboard in the kitchen.

Terrance was glad that she purchased these drinks. He opened the mauby and mixed it with cold water and added two ice cubes. 'Gyul, dis real nice. It feel like ah back in Couva.' He scratched his forehead.

Next morning, Nasha complained of feeling nauseous. Dorothy looked at Nasha and shouted, 'Yuh better not be carrying no damn child! I not minding no blasted child, you will put the child in a day care center or nursery or find someone to adopt the damn child.'

'Mommy…I might not be pregnant.'

'Ah know yuh pregnant!' shouted Dorothy, 'yuh vomiting in de morning and doh want to eat…I used to suffer from similar complaints. Why de hell yuh didn't use contraceptives? Her chest heaved and she took a deep breath. 'Ah not minding no damn child, put it in ah blasted orphanage!'

Terrance intervened, 'Listen, shut your stinking mouth woman and stop telling the child that. Yuh want she become traumatized like you?'

She was angry and expected her husband's support in the argument. It was stressful and she could not cope with the fact that she would soon be a grandmother. For her it meant that she was no longer young and attractive. She headed for the garage and drove off. She decided to go shopping to relieve the stress. She went to Western Beef and asked the cashier, 'Do you have a shelf with West Indian foods.'

'At the end of this middle aisle is the Ethnic Section. There are some foods and drinks there,' said the cashier who was a Ukrainian teenager. She and her sisters migrated to the United States in 2004.

Dorothy browsed the shelves and after ten minutes her cart had nine bottles of Cydrax, Chubby and Peardrax. She saw a bottle of Bitters. She was unsure if it was used for cooking or drinking but remembered that her husband regularly mentioned it. She checked to see if there were any security cameras focusing on her and then quietly placed the bottle in her handbag.

After paying for the goods, she went to the nearby store, Pathmark, and bought Rough Top and Ovaltine cookies. When she was younger these were her favourite. She returned home and dropped the bags of groceries on the kitchen floor. Her world was falling apart. Her hands were trembling and she had a throbbing headache. She checked her phone for a psychiatrist who did home visits.

During one of the counseling sessions, Mabel advised Dorothy, 'You should think about volunteering some of your time to help the less fortunate. Only then you would appreciate your life and truly understand the meaning of life.'

'Dat sounds so true. How I go begin dat sort of ting? I doh have no experience,' said Dorothy.

Mabel smiled. 'I have a friend who name Sumintra and she doing social work for more than twenty years. Here look her number.' She gave a piece of paper to her. After her patient left, she decided to take her monthly injection of Aimovig.

Dorothy carefully placed the paper on her refrigerator's door. It was held in place by two small magnets.

Next day, Dorothy met Sumintra at the entrance of a nearby mall. Sumintra was well-dressed and had an expensive handbag. She was smoking a Marlboro cigarette.

She was eager to show Dorothy how to be a well-loved volunteer. She took a final puff and threw the cigarette in a trash can.

Sumintra and Dorothy went shopping at Lowe's and had lunch at Chick-fil-a. Sumintra paid for the lunch and called an Uber. The taxi dropped off the women at St. Michael's Home for Special Children. Sumintra casually greeted the three nuns in the kitchen and introduced them to Dorothy. She proceeded into the dining room and patted five children on their heads. The children did not seem to recognize her. Sumintra became annoyed and shouted, 'Allyuh damn wretches too blasted ungrateful, I trying my best with everyone and this is the thanks!'

Dorothy had a shocked expression on her face. The nuns in the kitchen heard the insults but did not respond. They seemed helpless or accustomed to her boisterous demeanour. Dorothy took two pencils and three crayons and shoved them in her bag.

Three of the children were frightened when they heard Sumintra shouting and they began to cry. Sumintra ignored their reaction and continued, 'Ah hope you all keeping your hands to yourselves and not molesting anyone or hitting anyone.' She hugged a ten year old girl, with cerebal palsy, who was seated on a couch. The girl winced and pulled away. She had a spinal abnormality and the pressure of the hug was unbearable. 'You too! You is a real hypocrite…a real bitch. Is I who care for you and your stink brother when both of you was sick!' She looked at the other children and said in a sad voice, 'How everybody appearing so strange today? Allyuh making me feel bad in front my new friend who will be helping me from today. Her name is Dorothy.'

Dorothy slowly waved her hand. 'Hi.'

An autistic boy waved his hand and walked sideways to greet her. Sumintra shouted at him, 'Walk properly. Stop walking as if you are a damn crab.' The boy began to cry.

A six year old girl, with Down Syndrome, ran and hugged Dorothy who quickly unloosened the ribbon and clip from the girl's hair and placed them in her purse. Dorothy was quick and neither the girl nor the nuns saw the action.

Sumintra went to the dining table and noticed that one boy refused to eat the macaroni and cheese that the nuns had prepared. She twisted her mouth and frowns appeared on her forehead. She took the spoon on his plate and placed it near his mouth. He shook his head and did not open his mouth. She shouted, 'If you don't open you crooked mouth, I will slap and cuff your mouth till it open. You don't deserve to live. If you don't eat you will go to hell.' The boy did not understand and began to cry. She roughly placed her right hand on his cheeks and squeezed until he opened his mouth. Then she rammed the rice and chicken into his mouth. Two nuns ignored the action and Dorothy was frightened.

Sumintra washed her hands and then waved goodbye to the nuns and children. She exited the institution and Dorothy followed her. Whilst driving, Sumintra casually remarked, 'I always feel blessed after such moments.'

Dorothy was confused. 'What moments?' She opened a pack of Lay's and placed two potato chips in her mouth.

'Helping the less unfortunate. It makes me feel that I am making a contribution to society and helping create a better world. Those children would not know how valuable I am until one day I decide to stop taking care of them. This is my true calling in life- to help the less fortunate and the poor.'

Dorothy nodded and then asked, 'Do you take vitamins?' She took a map from the glove compartment and placed it in her purse. In the compartment were two vials of Percocet, a gun and a pack of Natural American Spirit cigarettes.

'Yes, lots of vitamins.' Sumintra smiled. She loudly cursed the speeding cars on the highway and did not notice the map being removed from the car's glove compartment. 'My husband is always warning me that I will die from a vitamin overdose similar to one of those cool artistes and famous Hollywood actors and actresses who die from drug overdoses.'

Chapter 7
Culture

Jose decided he wanted to leave his job at the airport and become an artist. At his first art exhibition he told Manuela Francisco, one of the patrons, 'My art deals with the common struggles of the Caribbean people. The fighting spirit was always there. We faced oppressive dictators, but it was our united actions in revolts, revolutions, marches and protests which broke the shackles of colonialism and imperialism. Last few years I have been painting scenes on religious and ethnic tolerance. There is a need for us to live in harmony and stop fighting among ourselves.' On the nearby table were packs of Twinkies, Baby Bundtz, Coffee Cakes and Zingers. There was an opened pack of Ding Dongs in his backpack. He had a chocolate addiction.

'Fantastic, that's amazing! What things or topics do your paintings represent?' asked Manuela. She was a Mexican who had relatives in Texas. She was enrolled for a Masters degree in Latin American History at the Center for Latin American Studies at the University of Miami. She hoped to teach at a university in the U.S. and later send for the rest of her family who lived in a slum in New Mexico.

A few viewers were captivated by some of his works. 'These paintings deal with regional unity, a fusion of ideas. The colours used on the canvas reflect religious, ethnic, cultural and political harmony,' said Jose.

Manuela pointed to two paintings on the wall. 'It's just utterly unbelievable that you can use the mediums of art to convey an important message for our peoples. But tell me, do people appreciate it? Are those paintings yours?'

'Yes, I have also incorporated religious symbols such as the cross, om, moon and crescent, such as these paintings to represent the world's major religions,' said Jose, 'you mentioned an important point about the appreciation of the public. Sometimes I have to reduce the price for my paintings to sell, and these are the original copies of my art. I guess that's why you always hear about the so-called starving artists.'

Manuela sipped a drink and continued, 'Is sad but West Indians and Hispanics do not appreciate their own culture. Instead of the youths reading the works of our poets and writers, they read Stephen King and Harry Potter books. And whole day they watching rubbish on cable tv.'

'Yes, but I have to continue producing work in the hope that it will somehow change somebody someday,' said Jose. He was frustrated and wanted to return to his former job in the airport. It was quiet and not stressful.

Manuela nodded. 'That is so true. I feel the same way. It is strange that I have been here awhile in this country and not met any Native Americans.'

He laughed. 'They blend in well…like the rest of us.'

She sipped her drink. 'I also do some voluntary work, giving lectures to schools and organizations on the importance of recycling, dangers of soil erosion, air pollution and deforestation. I feel they do not appreciate my talks but hope it will change somebody's way of thinking and there will be more concern for the environment here in the USA.'

Francine approached them and interrupted the conversation, 'Sorry to bother you señor and senorita. I belong to a group dat is collecting signatures for a petition which we hope to present to the prime ministers in the Caribbean.' She gave them sheets to sign.

Jose said, 'My English is bit rusty. Tell me what is writing here above names.'

Francine explained, 'Oh that simply states that the undersigned citizens of the Caribbean fully support any effort of Caribbean unity and pledge ourselves to continue building the region. It also demands that there be an end to racism, religious discrimination, unemployment, inefficient state corporations, corruption and nepotism. Jobs must be given to persons on merit.'

'Those are excellent objectives. I like to sign also,' said Manuela. She took a cupcake from a waiter. 'How many people are in your group?'

'My group has about twenty persons and we meet on a monthly basis,' said Francine, 'it was formed six years ago in Trinidad. It's a voluntary group yuh know like a non-governmental organization.'

'How many names have you collected?' asked Jose.

'About two million names.'

Both Manuela and Jose had surprised expressions. Francine wrote numbers on a piece of paper. 'Here is my cellular number. Give meh a call if yuh ever interested in visiting Trinidad. Maybe ah could organize an art exhibition or poetry reading for allyuh. It always have tings like dat in meh country.'

'What is your profession? Are you a diplomat, politician or ambassador?' asked Jose. 'You look dignified and I admire your zeal to promote a united region.'

Francine blushed. 'Who me? Nah, I is ah simple newspaper vendor.'

'We all have a role, however small, to play in forging stronger Caribbean bonds,' said Manuela, 'we should not feel anyone has an inferior job or is not an asset to the society. Everybody contributes in their own special way.'

Francine nodded and bit her lower lip. 'That is so true. Lissen, thanks for allyuh signatures ah want to mingle a bit with de odders and geh some more signatures.' She took the petition sheets, folded each one and placed them in her purse.

'Adios,' said Jose.

'Adios señorita,' said Manuela.

Francine left them and met other guests. ‘So what are your latest conservation projects?’ asked Marc, ‘I’m heading for Mexico to educate the natives on preserving pyramids.’

Francine felt dizzy and nauseous. She was rushed to a nearby hospital. The doctor realized she was pregnant. She was shocked to hear the diagnosis.

There were two Trinidadians at the exhibition, Aboud and Ritchie. Since migrating to the United States, they had lost contact with each other. Aboud was unemployed. He was chewing and wore Lee jeans that dragged on the ground. ‘This food tasting real good, long time ah didn’t eat bread that not freshly baked.’

Ritchie was slim and balding. He purchased two of Jose’s paintings and placed them near a post. ‘Same here. Long time I eh eat bread. I eh see you in ages. Where yuh living in de USA?’

‘I was living in Los Angeles for awhile!’ said Aboud, ‘life up here in de USA real hard…real hard to survive.’

Ritchie nodded. ‘Is true talk. Ah tell people ah regret leaving Trinidad. Ah living almost like a street child, a nowherian begging on streets, dem rich tourists from the United States always sympathetic. Sometimes when things hard I put down a little tief. And de usual dodging of the police to survive.’

Aboud raised his eyebrows and smirked. ‘A big hard-back man like you comparing yourself to ah street child? Yuh eh have no shame? Yuh was a boss in Enterprise. Wha’ about yuh homeys from de block?’

‘Most of de boys get gunned down in Trinidad…a few up here. Larse year I went down to Trinidad to visit a few of dem in jail.’

‘Buh how yuh afford things like bus fare and rent?’ asked Aboud.

‘Bus fare? Man, dat is for de rich people. Last year for the Christmas holidays, I went on a life-raft, dat me and some friends build. And I travel furse class on the raft. De only difference is dat it eh have no nice air hostess to bring yuh lunch and drinks. I living in a public housing project.’

‘Life-raft? Man yuh crazy,’ said Aboud, ‘yuh eh fraid sharks.’

Ritchie laughed. ‘Nah. Dat is ah real good one, ah have to remember it to tell meh friends when ah return. So what you doing these days?’

Francine returned to the exhibition and after twenty minutes felt dizzy. She excused herself and went outside and began vomiting. She wiped her mouth and felt a craving for cigarettes. She badly wanted to smoke and at that moment did not care about her unborn child. She thought about having an abortion when she returned to Trinidad and Tobago. She did not want children because she felt that she would not have been able to travel. She viewed children as a burden and did not want to spend the rest of her life changing diapers and spending money on their upkeep.

‘I’m feeling like…ah escaped convict,’ said Aboud.

'Yuh joking? A good man like you.'

'No, is true.' He began coughing and grabbed a bottle of water. 'After I read all the books in the prison library I get bored and tell myself that I want some freedom now and excitement, yuh know.'

Ritchie asked, 'So yuh just walk away from jail?'

'Well the corrupt prison guards were busy during a storm.' Aboud took a sandwich from a tray. 'Look, in nearby Grenada about two hundred prisoners escaped when Hurricane Ivan hit.'

Ritchie was ignorant of the current events in the Caribbean but wanted to appear knowledgeable, 'Yes of course.' Suddenly he gasped and began to slap his chest.

Aboud was concerned. 'Boss man you okay?'

Ritchie coughed. 'Yeah….sometimes the pacemaker does give a trouble and I does need to hit it to jumpstart it.'

'That not sounding right. Is that de pacemaker from Trinidad?'

'Yeah, ah tink it need a new battery or something.'

'You need to change it and get one made in the United States.' Aboud wiped a tear.

As I was saying, de big groups like the Red Cross raising millions of dollars to help flood victims. The United Nations World Food Programme bringing forty tons of food including rice, beans, cooking oil and bread.'

'Yes, that World Food Programme always gives valuable assistance to poor, scrunting people in de Caribbean, especially Haitians and Cubans,' said Ritchie.

Jose was nearby and overheard the conversation. He decided to introduce himself and said, 'Hi, I am Jose and heard both of you talking about the recent natural disasters.'

Aboud smiled and shook his hand, 'Nice to meet you Jose. Congratulations on your exhibition.'

Ritchie also greeted Jose and said, 'Yes congrats, I bought two paintings.' He pointed to the paintings near the post. 'Yuh know what is also interesting that natural disasters tend to strengthen Caribbean unity. Look, the prime minister of Trinidad and Tobago promised to give $5 million to another country to help with relief efforts.'

Jose asked, 'Both of you so smart.' He sipped a tequila.

'All de time!' said Ritchie in a sarcastic tone.

Aboud said, 'Ah sure you know that a former prime minister of Trinidad gone to Cuba for some heart operation. And he also had an eye operation and now has 20-20 vision.'

Jose nodded. 'Yes ah read of it. Ah hope he doesn't become a Marxist and Communist.' Ritchie and Aboud laughed.

'Yuh see this is what unity should be,' said Ritchie, 'just because some people such as in Haiti speak French, people in Cuba speak Spanish and some speak English does not mean we isolated from the rest of the Caribbean that speak English.'

Jose nodded. 'Is so true. If you read our history, before Christopher Columbus came, there were no divisions. Yuh know, me and you could well form a political party and win with some of these ideas.'

'All yuh have my vote,' said Aboud.

'Nah, nah, nah not me and politics, it have too much ole talk, bobol and divisions…de people only want to skylark,' said Ritchie 'in some countries dey does form political parties often as if is something simple like planting peas or corn. By staying out of politics ah able to talk about unity and people does hear me.'

Aboud shook his head and smirked. 'Yes, all ah we is one.'

Jose laughed. 'Yuh could say dat again! Doh dig nutten. We is piece of the West Indian family! The English-speaking Caribbean should not only interact with Latin America in sports and to stop the illegal drug trafficking, but we need closer regional unity. Is the only way we could fight the enemies of poverty, bad sanitation and diseases. If we don't unite then we dogs dead.'

'True,' said Ritchie. His chest pain had subsided. He looked outside. The sun had disappeared and dark clouds were on the horizon. A storm was coming. He wanted to leave before the downpour began.

Jose asked Aboud, 'Yuh ever thought about returning to Trinidad with all the political oppression, poverty and unemployment?'

'Never,' said Aboud, 'I am proud to now be an American citizen. I cyah abandon dis great country which has some of the world's best baseball players, athletes and boxers. And dat place Trinidad have too much crime, too much gangs, tings real bad down there.'

'You are very patriotic,' said Jose. He took a drumstick from the plate and bit into it. He smiled. 'This tasting as good as KFC.'

Aboud laughed. 'Man, yuh is a real clown. Anyway, what about you Jose ever thought about returning to your homeland?'

Jose took another tequila and swirled it. 'I have relatives here in the USA but I rather return to Venezuela and struggle with my people for a good government.'

Aboud nodded. 'Yes Jose, people must STOP running to developed countries and STOP contributing to the region's brain drain. All de kidnappings and murders in Trinidad make me pack my bags and leave. Meh family have a contribution to make to dat society.'

Jose smiled. 'Yes, all our intelligent, creative and artistic minds tend to run off to North America and Europe. Some go after more money, others are attracted to better social services such as electricity and water.'

'Is funny dat most of dem leave good, stable jobs like teaching,' said Ritchie, 'when dey gone foreign dey ketchin' dey tail to make ends meet. Dey forced to work in three and four jobs in McDonald's, KFC, or as domestics for minimum wage. And dey livin' in a two-by-four apartment and freezing dey tail off. Some gorn for one month and if yuh hear de accent. And a lot of people abroad illegal waiting for years for green card. Not me and dat life. Ah like sweet Trinidad and the warm Caribbean sun. So bro what are your future plans?'

'Man, ah have big plans, first ah planning to have an international conference of all the world's escaped prisoners. Then after dat, ah want to be a volunteer to assist with those affected persons who lost their belongings, homes, crops and animals during massive flooding in Jackson in Mississippi and Dallas in Texas. I feel August 2022 is a time for me to educate them on the dangers of flooding,' said Aboud. He sipped a drink and wiped his mouth.

'Yeah pal, best of luck. Ah admire yuh work.'

Francine realized that she could not stay away from alcohol and cigarettes.

She thought about the abortion. 'Let's go for some more drinks. Ah hope de people have oil down, sea moss or soursop punches. After de drinks ah goin' and sleep, ah feeling half-dead. Next Tuesday ah going to Labor Day celebrations.'

It was a chilly day. Francine arrived early for Labor Day in New York. She had a thick green sweater and a woolen cap. She recognized Aaron and walked towards him.

Aaron was chatting with Duke, a tall African, from Zimbabwe, who was wearing a jeans and jersey. 'I am Aaron. I am one of the sponsors of Labor Day.'

The Afro-American shook his hand and recognized the accent. 'You Trini?'

'Yeah, ah living up here now.'

Francine approached both men. 'Hello Aaron, yuh remember me? We met in Grenada.'

Aaron hugged her. 'Yes of course. Is good to see you again!'

She turned to Duke and shook his hand, 'Mr. Handsome, ah from Trinidad and Tobago. So tell me about yuhself.'

'I might look like an airhead but I got four PhD degrees, a law degree, two MBA degrees and I'm a professional dancer. I'm attached to the Malonga Casquelord Center for the Arts in Oakland. It's my sixth time in Labor Day,' said Duke, 'I've been helping other Trinidadians organizing events such as the Broward Caribbean Carnival, Miami Carnival, the Caribbean-American Carnival in Tampa, Boston Carnival and the West Indian American Carnival. I had helped Carlos Lezama during the 1960s and 1970s to have Carnival in Brooklyn. For two years I worked with Mas Makers Massive to help promote Trini Carnival in San Francisco for their annual celebrations.'

'You are amazing Duke. I am collecting signatures to promote Caribbean unity and solve social problems. Ah need allyuh signatures and some assistance in distributing them to the crowd tonight. Make sure de people return the pens and pencils,' said Francine, 'ah almorse didn't make it to Labor Day this year because ah didn't have a passport but luckily ah friend make one for me on time and loaned meh some counterfeit money.' She patted her hair and adjusted her blouse.

Aaron's phone rang and he checked the number. He reluctantly answered it. 'Hello. Yeah boss, it's no big deal. I too was shook when that pinhead clap up when the fuzz questioned him.' He paused. 'Boss, I aint no buck passer.'

Duke and Francine curtailed their conversation. They did not want to disturb Aaron.

Aaron gradually walked away from both persons. 'His brother is ah dead man walking. No sweat, he's salty and could only flex. Yeah chill. Will deal with both of dem.' He ended the call and placed the cellphone in his pants pocket. He looked at Francine and Duke.

Duke appeared embarrassed and continued chatting with Francine. 'Ah did read some newspapers a few weeks ago and there was a big advertisement about the movement to collect signatures in support of Caribbean unity. All de vagrants in my neighborhood support the effort. Doh worry all yuh head dem police is some real Babylon and only want to harass and lock up innocent people.' He wiped that was trickling down his forehead. 'So Miss Francine, for Labor Day will there be singers from Trinidad?'

'Yes, there will be artistes as Sizzla, Red Rat and Buju Banton. Tonight we will be having a private party with such Caribbean music as reggae, gospelypso, zouk and chutney.

The Caribbean and Latin America has proven to be the workshop of the world, especially with its abundance of talent and innovation.'

Aaron added, 'I think the common person on the street, the working class person, the grassroots person really like to hear Mase, Coolio, Beenie Man, Bounty Killa, Foxy Brown, DMX, Notorious B.I.G.'

'Yuh talking truth,' said Francine.

'You all must not feel inferior that you have seemingly minor jobs and not respected by most of society,' said Aaron. He lit a joint of marijuana. 'We have to ensure the USA is a safe, united and peaceful area. This is now our home. Sometimes I really missing chicken foot souse.'

'Okay the concert starts in ten minutes, let's go,' said Duke. He had a shocked expression. 'Is that ganja?'

'Yes de vibes good,' said Aaron. He smiled and exhaled. The smoke exited his nostrils like a dragon. 'The politically correct term is – medical marijuana. I'm allowed to smoke it.' He opened a beer bottle. 'So how many names yuh got tonight?'

Francine said, 'Almost 3,000 names today. This was a great idea to have this concert. Long time I eh wail down de place and geh on wild an' wassy.'

After the concert Francine left and took a taxi to the airport. After seven hours of flying she arrived in St. Kitts and took a taxi to the Hilton Hotel. Her main goal was to attend the Caricom meeting. They planned to present the petitions to the prime ministers. She attended a reception for some of the delegates and specially invited guests. Aaron was also in attendance. He helped fund some political parties in the Caribbean. It was a method of money laundering. Steelpan music was playing in the background. She entered a room filled with almost one hundred persons dressed in formal clothes. She mumbled to herself, 'Lawd, look how much people dey ram cram in dis very small room. It must be cost one set ah money to buy all dis food and rent this hotel room. Ah feel so low class. Meh mudder always say dat cockroach doh have right in fowl business.'

Wilfred, a CNN reporter, met Francine. He was a Trinidadian and began to chat with her. 'How are you marm?'

'I am fine.'

'Can I have a brief interview with you?'

'Yes of course, it's not a problem.' Suddenly, she blurted out , 'Ah coming back jus' now, ah going to de toilet…ah coming back jus' now.'

'Sure take your time, I'm waiting right here.' Wilfred smiled.

'Marm, would ya like a dwink?' said a short waitress who had a speech defect.

Francine raised her eyebrows. 'Dwink? A glass of mauby please.'

'Sorry, no mauby,' said the waitress.

'Okay, an orange juice then.'

The waitress looked at the roof and seemed thoughtful. 'Weef only have tings like water, Sprite, and Rum Punch.'

'Weef? Okay then, a Rum Punch,' said Francine. She was also hungry. 'I'm going to de toilet, when you bring de drink, jus' keep it for me…ah coming back jus' now.'

After fifteen minutes the waitress returned. 'Here you goes. What ya go like…like to eat?'

'It have any alcohol in this?' asked Francine. She expected a stupid answer.

'Ah not sure. It smelling non-alcoholic.'

Francine steupsed and asked, 'Yuh have rock cake or bake and shark? I feeling a lil hungry.'

The waitress quickly replied, 'Am, no.'

'Oh Lawd, ah know should ah never walk with meh two hand swinging.' Francine belched and patted her chest. 'Dis gas bothering meh.' She wiped her mouth. 'Yuh have saheena? Saada roti and talcarie?'

'Weef only have thuna and cheese shandwhishes,' said the waitress. She spoke quickly and avoided eye contact. She had problems interacting with people and this was due to Asperger's Syndrome.

'Shandwhishes? Okay, okay Miss Weef, a cheese sandwich go be fine.'

Wilfred returned from the washroom. Francine told him, 'Dat tie-tongue waitress speaking worse English than the Latin Americans I met. And, she lookin' force-ripe and she friends lookin' marasme.'

'Yeah she have a bad lisp.' He smiled and took a glass of punch from a waiter.

'EH, EH!' shouted Shelly. She wore a red dress, a green hat, blue high heels and on her arm was a purple purse. She embraced Francine. 'Matilda? What are you doing in St. Kitts?'

Francine pulled away. 'Ah sorry but ah feel yuh mistaken, I is not Matilda.'

Shelly was embarrassed. 'Ent you is de woman collecting signatures for a letter or something…to get rid of racism and unemployment?'

'Yeah is ah petition…buh meh name is Francine. Wait na…Shelly is you.'

'Yes!' Shelly blushed and reluctantly nodded.

Francine hugged her and introduced her to Wilfred.

Shelly asked, 'So what yuh doin' here?'

'Well, meh group collected almost three million names and dis evening a few members of my group will present it to the prime ministers,' said Francine.

'Three million! Gyul only who in de kitchen does feel de heat. Yuh deserve a medal for all dat hard work,' said Shelly, 'so yuh giving each leader all dem heavy boxes filled with signatures?'

'Nah we scanned the names and have them on these CDs. Here have one envelope with it.'

She accepted the envelope. 'Hear na, who give all yuh money for all de travels to the islands and for advertisements in the region's newspapers and radio?' asked Shelly.

'Some rich business people. One of them is Aaron, a Trini, who felt de need for unity as a solution to tackle de problems. He provided airfare and hotel accommodation, and money for the ads,' said Francine, 'he went to rest in the hotel room. Apparently he became sick after eating the cheese sandwiches they are serving. It must be old cheese or spoil bread.'

Shelly pointed to a serving plate. 'Yuh mean dem sandwiches.'

'Yes. Anyhow, ah goin' to dress up because this evening is de presentation of the CDs and I have to inform de odders of my group.'

Shelly nodded. 'Right, we go talk later. Doh forgeh I coming to visit later this year.'

The formal evening function began promptly at 7pm and the majority of persons were leaders of the various Caribbean countries. Francine and three members of her group were present. The group was to formally present the petitions to one prime minister who would then distribute them to the other leaders. There were elaborate plastic decorations near the podium. The prime ministers were seated around a table with microphones. Behind the table were national flags from the various countries.

'Fellow prime ministers and presidents, specially invited guests, distinguished ladies and gentlemen, let me cordially welcome you to this gathering of Caricom Heads of Government in St. Kitts. We have the Caribbean Court of Justice. This will mean we no longer need to rely on the Privy Council in Britain.' There was clapping from the audience. The speaker continued, 'There will soon be the implementation of the Caribbean Single Market and Economy, which will positively change our economies and better prepare us for globalization.' There was more clapping from the audience. 'We intend to strengthen the Caricom region and ensure that social, economic and political problems are resolved. The economic impact of last year's natural disasters will be felt for many years but it is through the collective efforts of other Caribbean territories that the devastated countries would be able to recover.' The audience clapped.

'The formation of the new trading block CAFTA- comprising Central American countries and the United States means that Caricom has to become more efficient and united. We need to examine the impact of the FTAA and the effects of such groups as the ACS and NAFTA on our economies. Today, before we begin formal discussions, there is a minor but noteworthy addition to the agenda. During the past year, a dedicated and patriotic group from Trinidad has been collecting signatures for a monster petition which supports Caribbean unity.'

Francine was thrilled. 'He talking about we, he talking about we!'

The chairperson announced, 'The group known as PURE will present to the leaders-a collection of CDs which contain almost three million names. I would like to call on a representative of the group, Francine to make the presentation of behalf of the group.'

Whilst walking to the stage, she patted her hair, fixed her dress and smiled at everyone. At the podium she gently tapped the microphone. TESTING, Testing ONE, TWO, THREE. On behalf of the people of the Caribbean and Latin America.' She was nervous and began to stammer. 'I, I, I would like to present these petitions to you, the honorable lllllleeeeaders of the Caribbean.' She paused and drank water from a glass at the podium and wiped her mouth. 'Dddeeese petitions are indicative of the desire for unity among the Latin Americans and Caribbean people. Doh only expect handouts from...people...and…de IMF and World Bank to always help wit' we problems… and all yuh doh run from the region.' There was light clapping from the audience. 'Now is de time for unity…and, and, and… let's join hands and build it, remember- is we Caribbean and Latin America. We the people of the region solemnly pledge to dedicate our lives to support our leaders' efforts in building closer, friendlier communities and countries.' After the speech, she presented an envelope to a prime minister.

She returned to her seat and asked Aaron, 'So how was meh speech? Ah planning dat for the last few weeks.'

'Everything was perfect. Like a speech at the Academy Awards. You sounded like a politician or Hollywood actress. You ever thought about entering politics or acting in the movies?'

She blushed. 'Fuh true? Na, not me and politics, I like to serve de people on de ground. Not me and dat fast lifestyle in Hollywood. Yuh really tink dat it was a good speech?'

Aaron smiled. 'Of course, I doh mamaguy yuh. Yeah we country go be proud too bad.' He patted his chest. 'I proud to be from de Caribbean.'

Chapter 8
A boring conference

'United States of America is the greatest civilization ever created,' said Fatima Salima Hosein. She resided with her daughter, Krystal, in Oklahoma. Every morning she would pray for her daughter who she boasted was a gift from Allah. Krystal was fifteen years old and was deaf. Her mother did an online course so she could communicate with her daughter.

Fatima was a Muslim refugee from Guyana. She migrated to the United States in 1973 during the oppressive regime of Forbes Burnham. Her father was killed in the Jonestown Massacre in 1978 in Guyana and her mother was from Aruba. This incident resulted in her family converting to Islam. Her brother-in-law was a professor at the Imam Khomeini International University in Iran. Her ex-husband was in a federal prison for two years.

The discussion was unfolding in Starbucks. This was the evening conversation prior to a well-advertised academic conference. Some of the speakers and registered participants decided to meet in an informal environment and discuss a few of the issues that were to be addressed in the conference. They were all eager to attend tomorrow's international conference at the Latin American and Caribbean Studies Center at Florida International University in Miami. The theme of the conference was- 'Media, Religion, Culture and Globalization: Impact on the Caribbean and its Diaspora.'

Fatima took a gulp of the caffè latte and wiped her mouth. 'The United States is much better…more advanced than the Ancient Egyptians….' She froze. Someone resembling her ex-husband entered the café and purchased two muffins. The man received his change and receipt and departed. The others seated around the table were surprised to hear this from a Muslim immigrant. After twenty minutes, the group ended their chat and left Starbucks.

Hans von Bismarck was a professor in Sociology at Waterloo University in the province of Ontario in Canada. His parents migrated to Canada in 1932 to escape the rule of the Nazis. They returned to Germany in 1947. Hans spoke in a loud voice. After he completed his cappuccino and placed the cup on the saucer. It was his third time in the United States but first visit to Florida. He still had his name-tag from a recent Cultural Studies conference at Howard University in Washington.

Manuela, the next speaker on the panel, twisted her mouth. She paused to collect her thoughts and rambled for her allotted fifteen minutes.

'Where does culture originate? What is the culture of United States?' asked Mala. She had seen the media conference advertised online at H-Net, and submitted a proposal which was accepted. She was excited. It would be her first presentation at an academic conference. On arriving in the United States in 1994, Mala worked for minimum wages at Sears, Geico and Vonage. After ten years of studying part-time and working, she decided to pursue full-time studies. Her husband, Alfred, was a real–estate agent and also sold life insurance. He was born in Switzerland and migrated to United States in 1983. They met through the online dating agency- eHarmony.com. Alfred had two daughters from his first marriage and both girls were gainfully employed. One of his daughters worked as a computer programmer at the governor's office, whilst the other was a musician.

Hans raised two fingers to indicate he would attempt to answer Mala's question. 'Culture could mean behavioral practices which are mimicked by which symbolic meanings are adopted. Culture is derived from the very beginning of a nation's history.'

Mala nodded and added, 'Indeed, with later developments in mass communications, relationships are no longer embedded in face-to-face interaction and thus the media plays a vital role in transforming cultures throughout the world.'

Jamal Shabazz was a Black Muslim. He was a follower of the Nation of Islam. He joined the group in 1992 and was one of the main organizers of the well-publicized Million Man March in Washington. His father was part of the March on Washington in 1963.

During the past decade, Jamal suffered bouts of depression when he lost custody of his daughter. He was a graduate of Michigan University and in 2007 completed a certificate program at the university's Center for Latin American and Caribbean Studies. On evenings, he enjoyed watching reruns of The Fresh Prince, Sanford and Son, The Jeffersons, The Proud Family, Family Matters, Good Times, Diff'rent Strokes, House of Payne, The Cosby Show and The Steve Harvey Show. These shows made him laugh and became part of his daily therapy. He had been listening attentively to the previous speakers and decided to make an input.

Hans scratched his head and looked at his fingernails. There were flakes of dandruff which caused his scalp to itch. He tried the anti-dandruff shampoo- Head and Shoulders, but this partly alleviated the problem. He wanted to try a shampoo with tar but did not like the smell of these shampoos.

Jamal wiped the corners of his mouth with a napkin. He now felt his time at Michigan was not wasted. 'The negative portrayals of West Indians and Latin Americans in the movies are the major way in which the U.S. has sought to convey and reinforce its cultural dominance.' His diatribe continued for five minutes. The conference ended, it was another grand talk shop.

A few of the participants and participants from the conference briefly convened at a nearby café. It was 1.30am. The conversation was stimulating and there was no sign it would end soon. Outside the shop, two homeless women were fighting and cursing. They momentarily stopped as a police car turned into the street.

Manuela was hungry and wanted to buy a hamburger at Wendy's. She continued to use illustrations in her arguments. 'I agree with Jamal's earlier point, but it's not only Blacks being stereotyped. The Hispanics and other ethnic and religious minorities have been negatively portrayed.'

'Hollywood has been changing...slowly but surely,' said Jamal, 'not many people would remember horror movies with Blacks such as Blacula, or the western Posse. There were Blacks in the comedy Benson, look at the impact of Eddie Murphy and Martin Lawrence in comedy and Halle Berry in movies as Catwoman. And a few years ago, Chris Rock hosted the Academy Awards and he has also appeared in a few well-received movies.' He rubbed his eyes and yawned.

With venom in her voice, Manuela retorted, 'Distorted portrayals are normal attitudes in the United States. When was the last time there was a movie based on Latin Americans winning an academic scholarship? Beating the odds and becoming a doctor or lawyer? Or running for the president of the U.S?'

Jamal could not understand why Americans would want to forsake their dignity and privacy to obtain fifteen minutes of fame. 'Why would Americans want to ridicule themselves and appear on shows as Jerry Springer, Catfish, Divorce Court, Maury and Dr. Phill?'

Mala quickly responded, 'Yes, I always wonder why someone would seek legal redress on Judge Judy or Judge Mathis. Are these persons hoping to obtain cheap publicity at the expense of privacy? The antics on Popstars, Jersey Shore and Laguna Beach are obvious indicators of people craving attention. Other reality shows with an absence of intelligence and logic include Rock of Love, I Love New York and Flavor of Love.'

Dimitri Sideris was from Thessaloniki in Greece. He did not understand the United States. He completed a Bachelor of Arts degree at the Center for the Latin American and Caribbean Studies in Indiana University in 2002. He also completed a certificate program in Caribbean Studies at the University of Connecticut. His parents felt it was a waste of their money to send him to study in the United States. They felt U.S. universities were inferior and wanted him to study in Greece or Europe. At Indiana University, Dimitri met and became engaged to an Italian girl. Dimitri was not mesmerized with the U.S. media. He derisively scoffed at such shows that parade misfits and demented individuals who seek cheap publicity and a workout from the staged fights which the live audience enjoys.'

Mala glanced at the clock on the wall. 'Oh my God it's 2am! We have to go and sleep. Tomorrow I present my paper.'

The others agreed to end the conversation and continue the discussion after the conference. Before returning to the hotel, Manuela bought a Baconator from Wendy's and Jamal decided to purchase a large container of chicken soup from Applebee's and a chicken sandwich from Ruby Tuesday. The conversation had increased their appetite. Both Jamal and Manuela suffered from reflux. Jamal hurried to the hotel room before the soup became cold. One of the homeless women approached Jamal and asked for spare change. He scornfully looked at her and twisted his mouth. He did not see a poor, homeless woman standing before him. He saw a white woman and whites were considered his enemy.

The second day of the conference had a larger attendance than the organizers expected. Maybe this was due to the fact that it was Saturday and some persons would not be at work. The registration fee of US$75 for students and US$100 for the public was not a deterrent and the turnout was partly due to the calibre of advertised speakers. There were two speakers from Warwick University in England and Oberlin College in Ohio. The auditorium could accommodate three hundred persons. There were nine persons from a West Indian group in Broward County in Florida. At the back of the auditorium, men were adjusting the sound and lighting systems.

There were two lines at the registration desk. Two female assistants, of Korean descent, were accepting money and creating name-tags for each registered participant and speaker. At the corner of the desk was a copy of the program. Dorothy was one of the participants but did not pay the registration fee. She was able to steal a conference bag, a bottle of coffee, five pens and seven notepads.

The first panel dealt with the impact of the media on masculinity. There would be three speakers and each had a time limit for twenty minutes. The chairman started promptly at 9.05am. On the table were five bottles of Zephyrhills spring water.

Mala would be the first speaker. She was excited and anxious. 'One of the characteristics of North American and European masculinities is that these are measured by status, wealth, power and success.'

Phillipe Rodriguez was seated in the fourth row and nodded his head. He thought about the various brands of Mexican rum that he had in his suitcase- Don Julio, El Milagro, El Guerrillero, Corzo Tequila blanco and Sangrita. He was a former alcoholic. He was eager to return to his hotel room and hoped the cleaner would not interfere with his suitcase.

Mala pointed to members of the audience as she spoke, 'Another popular illustration is the use of male athletes to advertise sports gear such as running shoes and clothes.' Dorothy glanced at the other members of the audience. She was bored. Pedro Gonzales, the chairperson of the panel, glanced at the clock on the table. He signaled that she had five more minutes. He felt Mala's presentation was not academic and her examples of movies were childish.

Mala ended her presentation and returned to her seat. She poured herself a glass of water and sipped it.

Pedro invited the audience to ask questions or make brief comments. He was the director of the Center for Latin American and Caribbean Studies at Duke University.

'Who is to blame?' asked an elderly lady with a walking stick. She pointed to the rest of the audience. 'Should others in society be held accountable?'

Mala quickly responded, 'Obviously, the tobacco, alcohol, song and television companies are concerned solely with profits and not the welfare of the consumers and the impact of an abuse of their products on developing societies.'

Hans was the second speaker on the panel. 'Defenders of the media might argue that movies and television shows are part of the culture or a work of art. Then it seems that there is a very thin line which separates entertainment and cultural rubbish. He turned a page and spoke louder. 'The annual Emmy, Grammy, Academy, Video Music and Screen Actors Guild and Golden Globe Awards are beamed around the world. This unnecessary annual hype is an attempt to indoctrinate the world, into accepting the decadent U.S. sub-culture as being refined and civilized. He was interrupted by some clapping. It was the first time that his presentation generated this response from listeners. He occasionally glanced at his speech.

Some persons smiled on hearing the familiar names of shows. After his presentation the chairperson invited questions from the audience. Nobody seemed interested then a middle-aged man raised his hand. Pedro allowed him to speak. The man gingerly approached the microphone in the aisle. He sought to defend the United States. 'The U.S.A culture is a free one. There are limits but freedom of expression is present. We don't force the Caribbean or Latin America to adopt our culture it is they who find it appealing.'

Manuela whispered to Hans, 'I'm trying to find a copy of of TVnotas, TVyNovelas, TVymás and TVTeleGuía. Have you seen any in the stores?'

He shook his head.

Mala gestured towards Pedro who allowed her to speak in the portable microphone on the table. She cleared her throat. 'Even worse is the fact that many lack the ability to distinguish reality from fantasy.'

Manuela bent her head backwards and drained the remnants of the cup into her mouth. The room was cold and she buttoned her sweater.

Pedro watched the clock on the wall and then thanked the speakers. He asked the audience if anyone had questions for the speakers. A Korean lady raised her hand and caught the attention of Pedro. He motioned with his hand for her to use the microphone in the aisle. She had silver hair and identified herself as a librarian from Fordham University. She had an odd accent. She questioned why there were so many Hollywood stars being convicted for drunk driving.

Mala smiled. It was an easy though irrelevant question. 'Just as some academics have MBA or PhD after their names, some of the over-exposed actors and actresses have DUI after their names! Some of these stars from Hollywood have graduated cum laude from the Betty Ford Clinic. They never fail to disappoint their fans.'

There were some guffaws from students who were near the exit door. The Korean remained serious and returned to her seat. Pedro cleared his throat and asked if any other members of the audience had any comments or questions. A participant, Joshua O'Brien, raised his hand. He was at the back of the auditorium and confined to a wheelchair. He had fractured both legs in a failed suicide attempt in 2002. The tragedy occurred after he learnt that he contracted HIV during the annual Spring Break in Mexico. He was a final year undergraduate student at Dartmouth College and was of mixed ethnicity as his father was Irish and mother was Scottish. He claimed to be an agnostic. His parents hoped that as an adult he would begin to attend church and believe in God.

For the past fifteen years Joshua was a collector of comics. He did not separate his hobby from his academic studies. One of his term papers dealt with the portrayal of American families in comics. He clutched the microphone in a clumsy manner as if it was a drumstick. After making his contribution, Joshua slowly wheeled himself to the back of the room. The ramp was steep and Joshua's arms were sore. He wished someone had brought the microphone to where he was sitting.

Hans yawned and grimaced. He was bored. Pedro watched the clock again and then announced, 'There will be a ten minute interval to refresh ourselves in the hallway.'

During the coffee-break some of the speakers mingled with the participants. There were doughnuts, cookies, juices, coffee and tea. Vishnu Balraj, a Guyanese who resided in Virginia, stepped outside to eat a packet of fries. For the past ten years he was a journalist for an online newspaper and his first novel would soon be published. He felt the coffee and biscuits at the conference were not enough to whet his appetite. His hunger was due to the fact that he skipped breakfast. He went to the nearby store and purchased a milkshake and two blueberry muffins at Dairy Queen.

The conference promptly began after ten minutes. The room was almost empty. Some of the audience were not interested in the speakers on the next panel or were still busy chatting in the hallway. The glasses and the three water jugs from the speakers' table were missing. The two microphones were missing. Dorothy was also missing and nobody realized she was the culprit.

The next panel focused on the media and its influence on society. Priscilla Callaghan, a British lecturer from the Caribbean Studies Department at the University of North London, sympathized with the victims of the media. 'I genuinely feel that part of the blame for today's problems is the hollow and puerile minds of script writers, television producers and distributors.' She stopped and adjusted her spectacles. 'These perpetrators are myopic and see only dollar signs at the box office. Hollywood has technology, equipment, human resources, millions of dollars but a drought of ideas.' She looked at the audience and sought to determine if there were any negative responses to her statement. Everyone had blank expressions. She did not see the man seated at the corner of the room who disagreed.

Patricia paused and drank water. Mala did not return to the auditorium. They remained in the corridor with a few others who were still enjoying the light refreshments. Dorothy deliberately collided with Jamal. This allowed her to steal his wallet.

Jamal quickly swallowed a mouthful of doughnuts and entered the auditorium. Mala began to discuss the underlying influences of the public's perception of beauty.

'The winners of beauty contests in India do not resemble the majority of typical brown-skinned women of India. Instead, the victorious women are those whose height, physical features, complexion and height fit into the Western ideals of beauty,' said Kavita Ranatunga from the Department of Consumer Studies at the University of Peradeniya in Sri Lanka. She was the next panelist and was on a sabbatical at Florida Atlantic University. In 2006 she gave a guest lecture for the Latin American and Caribbean Studies program at Rollins College in Florida and was a Fulbright Scholar at the University of California.

Mala was feeling hungry. She was trying intermittent fasting and skipped breakfast and lunch. She had joined a Dance Empowerment Group in her neighborhood. Her son taught ballet for boys at Baltimore County's Sudbrook Arts Center. During the lunch interval some of the participants went to nearby food establishments.

Joshua entered Starbucks and spent a few minutes browsing at the selections on the wall. He ordered a tall frappuccino juice blend.

The cashier asked him, 'Tall, grande or venti?'

He checked the list of drinks and decided on a grande. He paid and looked around for a table. He recognized one of the speakers chatting with someone. He decided to interrupt the conversation, 'Congrats on a fine presentation.'

Mala looked up and smiled, 'Thanks. That was an intelligent comment you made during the question time. Come join us.'

There was a momentary pause as the chair's legs scraped the floor. He asked the group if they could tell the difference between Pepsi and Coca-Cola.

Mala was the first to answer, 'Nope.'

'That is merely a gimmick. Both have the same amount of sugar, coloring and acid,' said Hans, 'it's like cigarettes. Different brands, different prices- but same cancer.' He was a former chain smoker who once enjoyed such brands as Salem, Winston, Camel and Rothmans.

Fatima nodded and added a new spin to the conversation, 'Similarly, nobody could tell the difference among hamburgers from Burger King, Wendy's and McDonald's. But don't dare say that to an employee from those places.'

'So Fatima do you agree then that all this hype about one tasting better, being healthier, is just gossip?' asked Mala.

'Yeah, the only difference is a few cents or dollars.' She checked her cellphone. It was a text message from her daughter.

Mala looked at Fatima. 'Excuse me I want to try the nonfat iced vanilla latte.' She left the table and headed for the counter. After one hour the speakers and participants wanted to return to the conference's venue.

Joshua continued his analysis of comics. He felt that more time should have been allocated for responses from the audience. At the end of the conference, some of the participants decided to return to their hotels and meet at an eatery at 7pm where they could discuss the day's topics. Five of the participants decided to meet at Taco Bell.

Amrita Beharry returned to the hotel and took the elevator to the sixth floor. She was a research assistant at the Center for Latin American, Caribbean and Latino Studies at the University of Massachusetts. Her father was an Indo-Jamaican and her mother was a Native American. Amrita and her two sisters were born in Atlanta. She changed her clothes and began checking channels for something interesting. There was a documentary- Super Size Me that was similar to a book she read a few years ago. She could not remember the author.

Fatima entered the 7-11 store to purchase bottled water. On the shelf were five different varieties. She looked for the cheapest brand and took two bottles from the shelf. She also bought the latest issues of Vanity Fair, Vogue, Elle, Bazaar, Good Housekeeping and Cosmopolitan. She purchased a pack of chewing gum and mints for her daughter.

A bookstore specializing in used non-fiction books attracted the attention of Jamal. He was a voracious reader. He began reading a variety of books whilst serving a two year jail sentence for tax evasion in 1986 and 1987. It was in prison that he embraced Islam. He decided on two books- The Chalice and the Blade and The Clash of Barbarism: September 11 and the Making of the New World Disorder. The prices were reasonable.

Before returning to the hotel, Manuela visited a mall to buy perfumes and colognes. She returned to the hotel an hour later with four large bags containing two blouses and bottles of Chanel, Ralph Lauren, Elizabeth Arden, Yves Saint Laurent, Lancôme and Aramis and Dior. She noticed a shoplifter with perfumes and alerted the security guard. However, it was too late. Dorothy had again escaped. The other members of the group were surprised that Manuela had such an expensive taste in fragrances.

Mala laughed. 'You could have spent some of that money on fries.'

Manuela smiled, 'Yes, that's a good idea. In Mexico there are many magazines catering for the needs of women. These include Siempre Mujer, Glamour, Vanidades and Marie Claire. These contribute to the women being fashion conscious.' She flipped through a copy of Rolling Stone. Near her elbow were two magazines, Twist Magazine and Life and Style Week.

Francine closed the door of the hotel room. She checked under the bed and behind the bathroom door. She was relieved there were no intruders. After showering she sat on the bed and opened a nearby drawer. There was a Bible. It was placed in each hotel room by the Gideons International. She placed the Bible in her suitcase.

Next day, there were three speakers on the first panel. Ishmael Kissinger was a Jew from Jerusalem. He was forty-three years old and a professor at the Center for Latin American and Caribbean Studies at the University of Wisconsin. His doctoral dissertation focused on Jews who sought refuge in the Caribbean during World War Two. He had recently divorced his Caribbean-born wife, Rebecca, who wanted to wear shorter, fashionable dresses and began flirting with younger men. 'Many consumers are not aware of the role of advertising and its subliminal messages which are not to inform but to persuade potential consumers to purchase and continuously use products. During the past decade women have begun to view themselves differently. This is a direct result of the influence of U.S. magazines.'

Fatima felt guilty whenever she purchased beauty magazines. She was a regular reader of these magazines since she entered the United States. Fatima's sister, a teacher at a private college in Michigan, had encouraged her to subscribe to TIME and Newsweek magazines. However, Fatima claimed that she never had the time to sit down and read the articles. She would look at the covers and that was sufficient for her to understand what was important for mainstream America. She purchased five magazines and a toy for her daughter. She checked the time and hurried to the conference.

Ishmael continued, 'Females are becoming more assertive, self-conscious, revealing and fashionable.'

Amrita disagreed with his view. She was the second speaker and was nervous. It was a controversial topic.

Manuela was bored and left to go shopping. She was hungry and wanted a vegetarian taco. The air-conditioned shop made her shiver. She regretted not bringing a light sweater and struggled with three large bags. On the outside of the bags were the names of two popular stores- Macy's and JC Penny. She had smaller bags with Estée Lauder, Neutrogena and Clinique. She checked her wristwatch and descended a long flight of stairs to the subway. She pushed open the doors of a toy store and browsed the shelves. 'Marm you have plenty Barbie dolls but do you all sell black dolls?'

The clerk was uncomfortable. 'No, I don't think so.'

'What about dolls looking like Asians?'

'No.' He adjusted his spectacles.

'Hmm. Ok. You have any dolls representing Caribbean folklore like douen or lagahoo? Is for a niece who birthday is next week.'

The clerk appeared to be thinking. 'No, we don't deal with that.'

'Next time I come in here, you all better have more dolls…or else I will sue you all.' Manuela stormed out the store.

Ishmael remembered a discussion at a rumshop in Grenada. He wanted medication as Viagra, Cialis and Levitra or Enzyte. Fatima wanted to make a contribution to the discussion but she was exhausted.

In the afternoon, Naima Selounski emerged from Burger King where she went to purchase a double cheeseburger. She was a Russian and received funding for airfare and accommodation from the Russian State University for the Humanities in Moscow. She was a lesbian but did not disclose her sexual identity to anyone at the conference. She stopped at a newspaper kiosk and purchased a copy of USA Today then joined the group at Taco Bell. The headlines dealt with an election race. She greeted everyone and seated herself next to Fatima.

Naima was excited. 'Television shows such as Desperate Housewives, Gastineau Girls, Sex and the City, Secret Lives of Women and Ally McBeal have negatively impacted on women. They want to showcase their newfound brand of sexuality.'

Ishmael did not agree with her view. Alexei Douglas of Jawaharlal Nehru University was among the group. Jacque Dominique, a cross-dresser from France, was one of the speakers scheduled to speak on the second day of the conference. He spent two years working as a hairdresser in Martinique and six months as a fashion designer in Guadeloupe.

Ishmael chose his response carefully. He did not want to offend Jacque and Victor Torero, a homosexual, who was a tenured professor from Spain.

Victor and Naima did not agree with the comments of Ishmael. Victor raised his hand to stop Joshua.

Alexei looked at Victor and Mala. Joshua loosened his tie and passed his hands through his hair. Alexei was not impressed with the facts from Joshua. He was perturbed that his contribution was cut short. Alexei hid his discontent and continued.

'The quality of American television and movies seem to be from a scary scene from a television series – The Twilight Zone or The Dark Zone,' said Amrita. She took a sip from her cup of hot chocolate.'

Victor felt cold and rubbed the palms of his hands. He was concerned that the contributions lacked academic content. He did not understand the rationale of using random movies to judge society. Furthermore, he believed their responses were nonsensical. 'You need to define moral and religious values.' He looked at Amrita. 'It would mean one thing to you and something completely different to another person.'

'You are right. I meant the need for traditional value- such as no premarital sex, decent dressing, respect for elders, a sense of God-consciousness and no foul language.' Amrita shook her head. 'I agree that these values are absent from the lives of most children and teenagers. On a similar point to what you mentioned, you need to define decent dressing.'

Victor was not surprised that she did not adequately answer the question. Her flimsy response reflected her unfamiliarity with the topic and inferior education. Joshua said, 'We could spend the whole day asking for further definitions. Whenever I use the term decent dressing, I mean acceptable to most of society…modest.'

Jacque glanced at his oversized wristwatch and muttered, 'It's getting so late and I must have my eight hours of sleep. Everyone I am leaving to return to the hotel.' He waved his hands in an effeminate manner.

Naima and Dimitris decided to also end the discussion and return to the hotel.

'Yes, I too am very tired from today's proceedings,' said Jacque.

Dimitri nodded, 'I feel that I am still suffering from jetlag.'

Alexei smiled. 'I cannot sleep now I want this big dinner to digest.' He rubbed his belly. 'I will read this article and probably buy a Tazo Green tea latte from the Starbucks across the road and then I will return later.'

Gadahar entered a bookstore that was near the venue of the conference. He had a crazed look and began cursing. Most of the customers ignored his outburst. He opened his knapsack, took a loaded handgun and assault rifle and began shooting at customers. After he went to his car and drove off. Sixteen persons were killed and forty two were injured. He was arrested and at the trial, Gadahar's lawyers argued he was suffering from Post Traumatic Stress Syndrome. The jury freed him.

The second day of the conference began with fewer persons than the previous day's attendance. At the registration desk, two persons were discussing the shooting at the bookstore. There were an estimated fifty persons. Jimmy Ming, one of the organizers believed that Sunday was a day for church and this could explain the low attendance.

Pedro, the first speaker of the day, ended his presentation with a controversial statement. The second speaker, Jamal, reflected on the manner in which art imitated life. 'It is clearly obvious, for logical-thinking and sane persons, that children and teenagers constantly fed a daily diet of violence will eventually mimic these acts. The old adages seem appropriate—you sow what you reap and chickens coming home to roost.'

A few members of the audience reacted adversely to the statement. A man raised his eyebrows and rolled his eyes. Two middle-aged women stormed out of the room.

Jamal was not distracted. He continued, 'Heavy metal and rock songs carry satanic and xenophobic messages.' Three of the participants yawned. One teenager began biting his fingernails then nibbled the top of a pencil. He sensed the lackluster audience, ended his rambling and headed for his seat. He was shocked to see his ex-wife, Fatima, seated three rows behind him. The chairperson introduced Carla and invited her to make a presentation.

Carla, a nurse from Trinidad and Tobago, nervously walked to the podium and adjusted the microphone. This was her first conference. She opened her folder and glanced at the first page of her speech. She coughed and cleared her throat.

After the presentations the chairperson, Kathy Birju, allowed questions from the audience. Jamal was the first to respond to the contributions. Carla nodded and made brief notes. Jamal saw her writing and felt that his words were important. He spoke loudly and slammed his left fist against the palm of his right hand.

Carla was allowed to briefly respond. She glanced at the notepad as she spoke, 'Yes I agree with you.' She cleared her throat and again glanced at her writings in the notepad. There were no more questions and the speakers had no final words. Kathy solemnly thanked the speakers and the audience. She preferred analysis rather than the many examples of movies and television series.

At the end of the conference, some of the speakers decided to have a casual meeting and continue these earlier discussions. They agreed to have dinner at the nearby Red Lobster. Victor was glad because he wanted to sample the seafood especially the shrimps. He recently went online and joined Groupon and would be able to get a discount on this meal. They entered the restaurant and were greeted by soft music in a dimly lit room. A young waitress approached the group. 'Do you have reservations?'

Pedro was the first to reply. 'No, but we have a party of six. Could we get a table?' He looked around the room. There were five empty tables.

'Sure. One moment please,' said the petite waitress. Within five minutes everyone was seated at a table near a window.

Victor raised the topic of the media glorifying crime and violence. Pedro agreed and began talking but was interrupted by Jamal who had missed the last ten minutes of the discussion. He had to pray. Jamal's brother lived ten minutes from Red Lobster and his wife, Betsheba, was pursuing part-time studies to become a paralegal. She usually prepared the meal but it was difficult since her left arm was paralyzed in a car accident in June 2002.

Pedro was glad that Manuela was at the table with the group. He wanted to have a discussion with her. He silently browsed the menu and remained sullen. He did not like the manner in which Jamal had abruptly derailed his conversation with Victor.

Manuela wanted to cheer up Pedro. 'Che Guevara is probably the most admired of Latin Americans of the twentieth century. Images of Guevara with his trademark beret are one of today's popular fashion symbols. What do you think Pedro?'

He stopped reading the menu and was reluctant to accept Che as a hero. 'Not many of these young persons realize that Guevara achieved his goals mainly through illegal and undemocratic means. The murders, atrocities and violence tend to be overlooked as the myth obscures the truth.' The waitress interrupted the conversation as she took orders for the meals. 'It's probably a search for an identity.' He watched the long legs of the waitress.

'Or a fashion statement?' Victor asked. He leisurely turned a page in the menu and decided to order a platter with deep-fried shrimps.

Dorothy entered the food outlet. She sat at a table and after the waitress took her order, she glanced at the other customers. Nobody was watching. She grabbed the bottles of ketchup, salt and mustard and threw them in her bag. The waitress took another order before submitting the orders to the kitchen.

Victor left the group and headed for the washroom. He washed his hands twice and dried them on the small heater near the door. As his hands were drying he thought about the United States. He could not understand how a country could invent a toilet with a sensor which automatically flushes but could not solve the problems of race relations, unemployment and poverty. He returned to the table. He wondered if the United States or another country invented the sensors on the toilet. He hoped the United States had invented it.

Juan Barchiesi of Universidad Torcuato Di Tell in Argentina, was another member of this nocturnal group. He was eager to present his paper on the final day of the conference and did not focus on the group's conversation. His daughter was part of the first group of students who graduated from the Center for Latin American and Caribbean Studies at the University of Georgia. He stared at the sign with the food prices. These were reasonable and he felt the price of breakfast at the Sheraton Hotel was too high. Last night Juan decided to have a chicken sandwich and cup of coffee at Arby's and ice-cream at Dairy Queen.

Dorothy quietly departed the outlet. In the hotel's hallway she saw a newlywed couple enter a suite. They forgot their suitcase in the hallway. She quietly opened it and took a deodorant, wristwatch and passports.

The waitress returned to the table with a tray of steaming dishes and drinks. Everyone in the group was eager to eat their meals.

Juan wanted to share an idea which stemmed from one of his recent articles which was published in the Journal of Psychology. He stopped chewing and swallowed. He felt sleepy and yawned. He looked at the clock behind the cashier. It was 10.30pm. 'I'll see everyone tomorrow, I'm heading back to the hotel.' He said goodnight to the group and returned to the hotel. He called a friend who lived at Fort Lauderdale and spoke for ten minutes. Near the lamp was his electronic airline ticket. After browsing through his speech for ten minutes he took a shower and went to bed. He had no problem falling asleep.

Victor was glad that Juan had departed because it meant more time for him to speak. He was enjoying the lobster and after filled his plate with breaded shrimps. Pedro finished his cup with Pepsi.

Pedro did not like the anti-government and anti-United States slant of the conversation. He nervously looked around at the persons eating at Red Lobster. He wondered if anyone was from Homeland Security or an employee with the CIA or FBI. He finished his cup of tea and ordered another cup.

The air-conditioned room was very cold. Most of the patrons wore jackets. Manuela decided to order tea. She sipped it and spoke in a soft voice. 'There is also little faith in politicians who are corrupt, deceptive and constantly accused of nepotism. Developed countries should have intervened when thousands were dying from genocide in Rwanda, famine in Ethiopia and the U.S. should have gotten rid of that dictator Mugabe in Zimbabwe.'

Victor sipped his tea and said, 'The Global South must stop being cowards and hypocrites. They must play an active role in changing the course of international relations. They must reject the paternal autocracy which governs their relationship with developed countries.' He twisted his mouth and wrinkled his brow. He opened his mouth and emptied the remaining drops of tea. He stared at the two potted plants near to the entrance and wanted to appear as if he was not part of the conversation. He became uneasy when he saw a security camera on the wall behind the cashier. Jamal wondered if it was powerful enough to record the conversation.

Pedro moved his chair and slowly stood up. 'I'm tired after a full day. I need to go and get my beauty sleep.' He yawned, slowly covered his mouth and left.

The others laughed. Naima checked her wristwatch. It was 11pm. Tomorrow she had to buy three magazines- Playstation: The Official Magazine, GamePro and PC Gamer. Her son was a gamer and he regularly bought magazines which offered the latest news in the gaming industry. The two teenaged cashiers were talking to the waitress. On a nearby table, one girl was reading aloud a text message from her cellphone. Her friend was giggling.

Mario Albanese was a final year PhD student at Verona University in Italy. This was his third conference presentation during the past year. His doctoral dissertation focused on masculinity and the media in the post-World War Two era. He had a pack of Marlboro cigarettes in his short pocket. He was not social and sat at a separate table. He ordered a sandwich and returned to his hotel room.

Sumintra was seated at a nearby table. She arrived yesterday and planned to attend the conference. She was worried and wished her daughter had not married a prisoner. The group decided to end the conversation and head for the hotel.

Next day the conference began promptly at 9.30am. The first panel had Mario and Pedro. They were introduced by Donna, the chairperson. Mario nervously approached the podium. He scratched his ear and coughed 'Violent acts stem from the depersonalization which occurs due to prolonged and continuous exposure to violence in the media. Power and violence are eroticized in the United States culture and has become a cultural ideal. This is important in understanding the heinous acts of rape, domestic violence and indecent assaults against females. This seems obvious to many in society but unfortunately it seems that this vital message has fallen on deaf ears as the vast majority of media houses have continued to transmit violence.' After his presentation he slowly returned to his seat.

Pedro's presentation was long-winded and his conclusion was biased. 'Caribbean citizens and Latin Americans need to deconstruct value systems which portray violence as an essential attribute of the ideal man.' Donna placed a slip of paper on the podium. She had scribbled- 'Five more minutes.' She scratched her head.

He saw the note and decided to make a concluding statement

'Any questions from the audience?' asked the chairperson. Indeerah raised her arm. The chairman allowed her to speak.

'Yes, my name is Indeerah and I agree with the last speaker.'

Pedro nodded. He was casually dressed with a short-sleeved shirt and jeans. Victor did not like the content of the presentations and began to detest the conference. He felt last night's discussion at Red Lobster was more fruitful.

Yuri Molotov of Poland was employed in the media a crime reporter. He worked with the BBC during the 1980s. He was slim and wore a green long-sleeved shirt that seemed two sizes too large. His hair was neatly combed to one side.

The theme of the final panel was 'Sexual Freedom and the Media.' Yuri's presentation was on pornography. He sought to provide a historical context in his introduction. There was a murmur from the audience. It was a long-winded presentation that was incoherent.

The next speaker was Anand. He wished Hema had attended the conference because she had informed him of the event. His presentation was entitled 'Dark Secrets: The Impact of Porn on Society.' His dramatic opening statements caught the attention of the audience. There was a short intermission for juice and coffee.

Juan yawned. He had to return to his hotel to pack his suitcase. The check out time was 4pm.

Anand, Donna, Vishnu and Amrita departed the conference and headed for Pizza Hut. They ordered two large pizzas. One would be vegetarian and the other would have salami and roast beef. Amrita initiated the conversation, 'I blame the media for the state of America.'

Donna smiled and interrupted her. 'It is obvious.'

Amrita said in a defiant voice, 'We are powerless. We cannot change Hollywood and the American society.'

'So you want to just wash your hands of everything bad…just like Pontius Pilate,' said Anand.

She nodded. She was bored and began reading cellphone messages.

Donna interjected, 'Remember we cannot force religious shows and values on the public.'

'Well what type of shows do young people like?' asked Vishnu.

Donna replied in a sarcastic tone, 'Shows with supernatural stuff are okay. It would not offend anyone but don't talk about God.'

Vishnu twisted his mouth. He felt powerless. 'We are wasting our time and energy. Let's just accept society as it is- with all its problems. You and me cannot change the course of an entire civilization.'

'Especially if that civilization is the greatest that ever existed,' quipped Anand.

'Exactly!' Fatima did not realize he was being sarcastic.

Vishnu yawned and stretched his arms. 'We have to remember a considerable number of movies are historical in content. Not only the U.S. media has harmful effects but there are other foreign influences. This includes sub-titled kung-fu and karate movies which are imported directly from Asia.'

Donna added, 'The topic of Bollywood has potential for a separate conference.'

'It's true,' said Vishnu. He stared at the ceiling. He was not admiring its designs but was in deep thought. He wondered if they were really wasting their time as the conference seemed like another talk shop.

After pizza, the four persons left for the hotel. They entered the lobby of the hotel. Anand noticed the bell at the desk was missing. The bellhop and the receptionist could not understand how it suddenly disappeared. Dorothy had taken it. They headed for the elevator.

Chapter 9
Hoops and homecoming

Jamal migrated to Minneapolis in 2005. That morning he ate leftover fries and chicken from Sonic and checked the NBA scores. It was a close call, Hornets won with 98 points and Bobcats scored 95. His childhood dream of playing professional basketball was finally realized. His hero was Kareem Abdul-Jabbar.

The feeling of nervousness was in his bloodstream. He wiped the sweat from the palms of his hands. Five minutes later, he had the ball in hands and was aware that his legs were trembling. He focused on the hoop and threw. He missed. At the end, he scored ten points and went cold on offense for twenty minutes. It was one of his better games this season.

Jamal played for Timberwolves. In the game against the Suns, he had 33 points and five assists. He received the pass from Nikol Pekovic who added fifteen points and sixteen boards. His team was missing guard Rocky Pekovic. The Timberwolves earned their fifth straight victory at home. The Suns was on a losing streak.

Duke moved to Florida. He travelled to Milwaukee to play against Miami Heat. He was recovering from a mild case of food poisoning. His team won but would later lose to Bucks. He scored ten of his twelve points in the third quarter. At the end of the game, he had eighteen points, 10 rebounds and five blocks. In the previous games he had scored eighteen points and made seven three-pointers.

Jamal checked the results in Memphis. His former colleague earned thirteen points for the Grizzlies on 5-of-16 shooting. The team had outscored the Nuggets in the fourth quarter and had built a 67-48 halftime lead. He was a staunch supporter of Obama in the upcoming presidential elections.

Indeerah carefully crossed the road. She went to browse through magazines in the pharmacy. There were men's magazines in the upper shelf- Men's Health, Esquire and Muscle and Fitness. She was more interested in the lower shelf which had Self, Shape and Home. After forty minutes, she bought Better Homes and Gardens and Fine Cooking. She began walking among the aisles searching for Hershey's chocolate bars. She remembered reading about the health benefits of eating it. However, due to her diabetes and high blood pressure, she was reluctant to buy snacks and sweets. She stopped to read the label for a new product – Fairness Cream for Men. It was made by the Activor Corporation of USA. She decided to purchase it and was eager to apply some on her husband's brown skin.

She bought lunch at Whataburger and reflected on her recent achievements. She had completed an online degree program and after six weeks received a doctorate. She graduated as a clinical psychologist and began writing a book. She applied for jobs at the Rutgers-based National Marriage Project and at the Philadelphia-based Council for

Relationships. Both rejected her and she decided to offer online counseling. After five months, she had diagnosed persons as demented, introverted, delusional or eccentric.

Sumintra was a volunteer in an asylum. This was her first visit. She was nervous and unsure of the welcome she would receive. A nurse met her and asked her to sign forms and gave her a visitor's badge. She liked the badge it made her feel important. She followed the nurse to a room in which an elderly man was sitting in a chair. On the table was a plate with a glass of juice, and tablets.

'Here is Terrance. He is not violent and really needs someone to talk to,' said the nurse, 'He was a professor teaching Communication Studies at Rochester University. Two years ago he had a nervous breakdown due to a false rape case. Subsequently, his wife divorced him. Since then he has exhibited anti-social behavior. He does not like to talk or interact with the other inmates. He is very knowledgeable and if he is in a good mood he will have a good conversation.'

Sumintra smiled and said, 'Good morning.'

Terrance avoided eye contact. He was staring at a lamp on the table. Sumintra ignored his reaction. He remained silent and stared at his shoes. He bent down and tied the shoelaces. He stood upright and stared at the curtains, wiped it and cursed. Then after a long period of silence, he said 'The media cannot be trusted. Dorothy did you iron my shirt?'

Sumintra nodded. She wondered who was Dorothy and was glad to see he was talking.

He did not care about her reaction. He was energized and began to walk around the room. He pounded on a small mahogany table. 'Dorothy, I blame the New World Order for our decline. It's a global conspiracy.'

He paused and decided to stand on the chair. He watched around the room. 'Any questions?'

Sumintra remained quiet. She drank some of the juice. She thought it was for guests.

He continued the lengthy diatribe. His voice changed and he smiled. He cleared his throat and pointed to the window as if it was a screen filled with statistics, maps and diagrams. He passed his hands through his uncombed hair.

She wanted to interrupt the conversation but felt it would not be a wise decision. She stared at the watercolor painting on the wall. It depicted a scene during winter.

He shouted, 'UFOs are real! Aliens are among us!' He paused. 'Any questions?' He looked at the curtain, lamp, bed and painting. The room was silent. 'Good I will see you on Thursday morning and remember we have a quiz.'

He sat on the chair and stared at Sumintra. 'Marm are you from the media? New York Times or Washington Post? Did you come especially to interview me?'

She nodded. She saw two green tablets and wondered if these were for guests. She placed one in her mouth and chewed. It was bitter and took a mouthful of juice. He began lamenting about the failures of academia. Then he stood on the chair and began to discuss human suffering.'

Sumintra listened. She felt that he was intelligent and not insane.

Terrance paused and wiped his brow. He looked at the table and acted as if there were lecture notes. He appeared puzzled and then asked, 'Am I speaking too fast? Please tell me if I am doing that. Some of these lectures are online on my webpage. The visits to the asylum did not affect her. She took a green tablet from the plate and quickly placed it in her mouth. 'Class dismissed.' He took off his shoes and went on the small bed.

She opened the door and quietly departed. She felt like a high school student who did complete her homework.

In July 2012 there was a deadly shooting in a movie theatre in Colorado during the action film, The Dark Knight Rises. Bertrand and a friend were in the cinema. Both were lucky to escape unscathed. A few months later, on 14 December, there was a massacre at a school in Connecticut. Francine wanted to stay and collect more signatures but was afraid of the crime. Yesterday, in the New York subway a man was pushed on the tracks. Onlookers were too shocked to help and Aaron took photographs of the man before he was killed by the subway train. She was worried about the increasing violence and uncaring nature of American society. She read about the fiscal cliff but did not understand it. She was perplexed and believed the fiscal cliff was near Mount Rushmore. On 17 December, she decided to leave the USA and return to Trinidad and Tobago. Her friends and relatives were convinced that Francine was a deportee.

Upon returning to Trinidad and Tobago, she went to Carenage. It was a peaceful Saturday morning. She looked at the sun's rays dancing among the small waves. She thought about the unborn baby growing inside her. Each day this baby was becoming part of her. A teenager approached her and asked, 'Why is there all those plastic bottles, food wrappers, pieces of metal, old barrel and torn clothes in the water?'

She smiled and admired his boldness. She did not know why Trinidadians abused their environment. 'Young man, this is a form of advertising for companies. Sometimes it is too expensive to have advertisements in the newspaper, television and radio. Or it is too expensive to have billboards. So these companies pay people to advertise their products in the sea or rivers. Look see that KFC box, wrapper from McDonald's, Burger King, beer bottles and soft drink cans.'

The teenager nodded. 'Yes, I understand. Whenever I go to a river lime I notice how successful the companies are in water advertising.'

'Yes that's exactly what it is- water advertising.' She pointed to an old jersey floating near dead fishes. 'And over there somebody is advertising a brand name jersey.' She did not want to ill-speak fellow citizens who were uncaring and thoughtless. She continued staring at the ocean and after one hour decided to return home.

After discussions with close friends and relatives, Francine decided she would not have an abortion. She stopped smoking and drinking alcohol.

In 2023, Sumintra was disappointed that the world did not end. She was featured on Extreme Couponing. She was very proud to be on cable television. She had a pet pompek, Cookie, who was featured on that episode. She was very concerned about the health and safety of Cookie and ensured her pet received vaccines and regularly visited the veterinarian. In the grocery she bought the most expensive biscuits and chocolates for Cookie. She was careful to read labels for Cookie's food. She chose pet foods that had words such as 'low in cholesterol,' 'no transfats,' 'no preservatives,' 'no additives' and 'rich in antioxidants.' Few in the public knew the meaning of transfats. Sumintra asked another customer, 'What de hell is transfats?' The frightened customer shrugged his shoulders and quickly walked away.

She did not seem bothered and approached the cashier. 'Was transfats supposed to prevent cancer and reduce blockage of the arteries in pets?'

The cashier did not know. 'According to popular surveys all our products have transfats.'

Sumintra bought a new brush to comb Cookie's hair. She returned home and packed the groceries on the shelves. She took a tin of tuna and checked the expiry date. It had not expired. She opened the can and emptied the contents in Cookie's food container. After she took mineral water and poured it into Cookie's water dish. She checked the newspaper to see the winning numbers for the Powerball lottery. Then, she gave a pedicure to Cookie. She shouted at the dog, 'Behave yourself and stop fidgeting. You have Attention Deficit Disorder?'

The telephone rang. She rinsed her hands and answered the phone.

'Hello, Sumintra speaking.'

Vladimir said, 'Hello, it's me.'

Sumintra was disappointed. 'Yes. What can I do for you? Do you want money?'

He paused. 'I want nothing. How did you cope with Superstorm Sandy?'

'Yeah, it's been tough. Some parts here in New Jersey are closed off and we are lucky we are not in New York because it was badly hit. Trees are blown down and the subway is flooded.'

'Well I am glad to hear you are safe,' said Vladimir.

'Did I tell you that I have been recently diagnosed with Alzheimer and Parkinsons?' She admired her engagement ring.

'No. Is it serious?'

She yawned. 'Not really it's in the early stages. I'm not worried the health care system up here in the USA is the best in the world. I'm taking precautions. For instance, I have my name tattooed on my arm. So in the future, I would be able to always remember my name. I'm hoping to get my passport, bank account and social security numbers tattooed on my arms. This will make it much easier for me to have the information if I need it. Some days I forget these numbers and where I have these cards.'

'You should also have your cell number and important numbers as the police and ambulance tattooed on your body,' said Vladmir, 'I heard you got a recent tattoo.'

'Thanks for that advice, I will certainly do that. This tattooing is a wonderful experience and makes my life so much easier. The tattoo artist is very famous and some of his designs were featured on NY Ink. Almost forgot to tell you but I'm almost finished doing an online course. Soon I would be a fully qualified financial planner. I will be able to advise families and companies about cutting costs. I'm also being trained to do telepathy and telekinesis. Oh, I'm working as a volunteer social worker in an institution that deals with the physically and mentally challenged. Oh, there will be fundraiser to help my friend and I want you to buy tickets.' She looked at the clock on the cabinet. In two hours Dog Whisperer would begin. Every week she and her dog would enjoy watching it. She decided to save money to visit the Dog Psychology Center in California.

'For what? Is he or she ill?' asked Vladimir.

'None of your business.' She was collecting money to begin a superPAC to assist her son's future presidential campaign.

'How is the volunteer work?'

Sumintra quickly replied, 'Great. Last week I spoke to a professor who is supposed to have a nervous breakdown. But I really believe he is being brainwashed by the CIA or FBI because of his strong anti-American views on the media.' She sighed. 'It was like a scene from a Hollywood movie.'

Vladimir was serious. 'Are you sure…you serious?'

'Yes, yes…I not joking, it's not a conspiracy theory. The man is brilliant. He has an excellent memory and is working on articles and books. I believe he is pretending to be mad so the secret organizations will leave him alone and not harass him. I now realize that it have more mad and crazy people outside the asylum. And that is what is really frightening. Instead many more frightened by an invasion of aliens from outer space or doomsday.'

'I totally agree that there are more mad people outside the asylum. Last month, at the airport I met a woman collecting signatures in the hope of ending poverty, racism and unemployment. She is definitely mad and not living in reality. I told her that them things will never, never go away.'

'Everywhere have mad people.' She smiled. 'Look, I recently attended a conference in Florida and everybody blaming the media for problems in society. Professors with plenty qualifications talking real stupidness and garbage. You still supporting Trump?'

He sighed. 'Nope, I decided to give my full support to whoever is the Republican candidate.'

'Did I tell you that I will soon be marrying an American citizen soon?'

He did not seem surprised and loudly laughed. 'No. I assume you are doing it to get legal status.'

'Yes, he is an ex-president of the USA. You might know him.'

'An ex-president? Really who is it?'

'His name is George Washington.'

'You are a real social climber,' he said, 'I guess people will soon have to call you- Mrs. Sumintra Benn-Washington.' After a long pause he asked, 'Isn't he dead?'

'Yes, but I have not found any laws in this country that says you cannot marry a dead person. This is a great country where the dead do not face discrimination.'

He coughed and cleared his throat. 'Yes, dead lives matter.'

'Did I mention that I am pregnant?'

'Pregnant? Who you?' He was not sure if she was lying. 'Sounds cool.'

She wondered if he was jealous. 'Yes, you wouldn't know my new man…he's a migrant like myself. His name is Terrance.'

'I'm happy for you and Terrance. Anyway, I almost forgot to tell you that Ali and Indeerah are divorced. I visited Ali three weeks ago and he has a serious lung problem. He had previously been misdiagnosed as having a spinal abscess. He is constantly coughing and is diabetic. He is more than one thousand pounds now and is the heaviest person in the world.'

'I never really liked Indeerah.' Her voice lacked emotion. 'I wished he had never married her. She was never a good match for my son. Why did they get divorced?' She paused. 'He did not mention the divorce to me. Don't worry about the coughing he will grow out of it. I'm very surprised my baby boy is diabetic, he always look so healthy. If he needed advice on his marriage he should have called Miss Cloey de psychic on tv.'

'Ali said he wanted a divorce because Indeerah don't buy Charmin Ultra Soft toilet paper and that is the brand that he like….'

Sumintra interrupted, 'It damn good that he divorce that ungrateful fool. I want de best for my son. She should have bought the best toilet paper brand for him. De boy have a soft bottom. Who will help him get food?'

‘He hired a woman known as Dorothy but…I feel she is stealing his food. Did you hear that Jose is writing a biography on Ali? Also, some company from Hollywood want to make a movie about him. He will soon be featured on the National Geographic Channel.’

Sumintra was excited. ‘This is a great country! I am glad to see that unsung heroes like my son are finally being honored. Anyway my tv show will start soon. Goodbye.’

‘Right, okay have a good evening. Bye.’ He went into the kitchen, opened his laptop computer and checked online for the marriage laws of the United States. Next day he visited the local library to check other laws. He planned to marry the Statue of Liberty. He also wanted citizenship. If this plan did not materialize he would return to his homeland.

Two months later there was another shooting incident in Texas. Francine was glad she was no longer in the United States. She decided to destroy the list with millions of signatures. Her group soon became dormant. She was no longer optimistic and full of enthusiasm. She eventually accepted the reality- that poverty, unemployment and racism would always exist. She embraced motherhood and as a single-parent wanted to ensure her newborn son would be successful and happy.

Vladimir was contacted by Russian authorities to assist in the hacking of computers that would be used by American voters in the 2016 presidential elections. He was a secret agent posing as a lowly airport employee. His secret assignment was to hack the servers and to forward this information to WikiLeaks.

In August 2024, hurricanes damaged some Caribbean islands. Francine saw the tragic news on the television and newspapers. Her son was four years old and attending preschool. His father was Marcus. She thought about her Caribbean friends who had signed the petition and wanted Caribbean unity. Yesterday she received emails from Bertha and Jestina who resided in Grenada. She went into the kitchen and opened the cupboards. She decided to donate canned foods and pampers to relief agencies.

Sumintra was caught by Homeland Security and deported to Guyana. The authorities received a complaint and searched Sumintra’s apartment. They found nine high powered rifles, vials of holy water, eight rocket launchers and fifteen grenades. She told the police that the weapons were part of her preparation for the Zombie Apocalypse.

In November 2024, Ali died. His funeral was well-attended and his dream was finally realized. The Guinness Book of World Records included his name as the first person to be buried in the world’s largest coffin.

Manuela was worried that she would be deported. She was pregnant and the father of her child was Jose. She recently completed her undergraduate degree at the University of Miami and was searching for a part-time job. Her two brothers had illegally crossed the border and were working at a restaurant in Texas. Both were staunch supporters of Trump. On Sundays they would attend the Lakewood Church and enjoyed listening to the pastor- Joel Osteen. Manuela's brothers and Jose were hired to build the infamous wall to reduce the number of illegal immigrants. In 2024, her brothers returned to their homeland.

Printed by Books on Demand GmbH, Norderstedt / Germany